Learning Curves

Education Advocacy
for Children in
Foster Care

By Kathleen M. McNaught

with a Foreword by the Honorable Constance Cohen

Edited by Claire Sandt

ABA Center on Children and the Law

National Child Welfare Resource Center on Legal and Judicial Issues

...a program of the Children's Bureau

Washington, DC

ISBN 1-59031-408-5

This book was made possible in part through a grant to the National Child Welfare Resource Center on Legal and Judicial Issues by the U.S. Department of Health and Human Services, Children's Bureau.

The views expressed herein have not been approved by the House of Delegates or the Board of Governors of the American Bar Association or the United States Department of Human Services, Children's Bureau, and accordingly, should not be construed as representing the policy of the American Bar Association or the Children's Bureau.

Printed in the United States of America.

Library of Congress Cataloging-in-Publication Data
McNaught, Kathleen M., 1969–
Learning curves: education advocacy for children in foster care / by Kathleen M. McNaught; with a foreword by Constance Cohen; edited by Claire Sandt.
    p. cm.
Includes index.
Portions of this book appeared in a different format in ABA Child Law Practice, published by the ABA Center on Children and the Law.
ISBN 1-59031-408-5 (pbk.)
1. Foster children—Legal status, laws, etc.—United States. 2. Foster children—Education—United States. I. ABA child law practice. II. Title.

KF3736.5.M36 2004
371.825'4—dc22

                        2004016362

Portions of this book appeared in a different format in ABA *Child Law Practice*, published by the ABA Center on Children and the Law.

Graphic design by Diane Buric Design & Illustration, Silver Spring, MD.

TABLE OF CONTENTS

Foreword

On any given day there are more than 500,000 children in foster care placement in the United States. When the juvenile court system invades a child's life, a judge is charged with the duty to protect the child's safety and well-being. To fulfill that duty, the court must rely on information collected from many sources: the child, the child's parents, the child welfare agency, the child's advocates, the school, and direct providers, to name a few.

A judge who fails to recognize the important role of education in the life of a child from birth through adulthood may miss an opportunity that could alter the course of that child's life.

"Jack" is a case in point. Jack came into the juvenile court system as a 10-year-old child whose father was a methamphetamine addict and whose mother physically abused him. During the case, Jack appeared in court several times. He expressed his need for a safe and loving family. Jack and the judge spoke of many things: pets, motorcycles, and, of course, school. The judge requested Jack's school records. Jack's grades did not reflect his abilities, and the judge told him she was disappointed; he could do better.

In the meantime, Jack's attorney discovered his affinity for airplanes and arranged for a military pilot to spend time with him at the airfield. Jack had the opportunity to operate an F-16 simulator. The pilot emphasized the importance of math in his profession.

On his adoption day, the judge learned that Jack had raised all of his grades to As, except for a B in math. The adoptive parents thanked the judge for her interest in his grades because it was her conversation with Jack that had motivated him to study harder. They also thanked Jack's attorney

because it was the visit to the airport that prompted Jack and his adoptive father to agree to spend time during the summer honing Jack's math skills.

Jack's is a simple story. Every day in our child welfare system there are complicated scenarios that demand a working knowledge of more esoteric nuances of the world of education. Few system stakeholders are equipped to comprehend the significance of FERPA, the Chafee Foster Care Independence Act, IEPs, Part C of the IDEA, EPSDT, or a manifestation hearing. (Don't panic…the book will explain these acronyms.)

Yet without a fundamental understanding of these issues, how can those of us who are entrusted with a child's well-being make sound recommendations and decisions for the child?

Children who are removed from their families and placed in a stranger's home, with no warning, are children whose lives are turned upside down through no fault of their own. Who among us would thrive in an unknown place not of our choosing with mysterious rules, customs, sounds, and smells? We in the child welfare system have the power to minimize trauma by maintaining or obtaining educational stability and opportunity.

To meet the needs of our nation's most vulnerable children, noneducators in the system must first learn what questions to ask. This book will help assure that the children whose lives are entrusted to us have every opportunity to soar.

Judge Constance Cohen
Associate Juvenile Judge
Fifth Judicial District of Iowa

Preface

I will always remember my early days at Legal Aid as a new attorney representing children in the foster care system in Maryland. Within those first few weeks I received my first request from a caseworker to attend a school meeting with her on behalf of one of my clients. I spent the night before the meeting reading our office's IDEA manual and off I went. While I do recall my presence as an attorney at the meeting drew some attention and provided some benefit, I also remember feeling overwhelmed by the amount of information that was being shared, the acronyms that were being bantered about, and the feeling that my young 10-year-old client was being lost in the process.

During my remaining years at Legal Aid and my subsequent years in private practice, my knowledge of education law increased. The more I learned, the more I wished I could turn back time and use my new knowledge to do more for some of those early clients. This book is the culmination of two of my greatest interests: to improve the lives of youth in the foster care system and to ensure that these youth receive quality educations that will help ensure a bright future. My wish is that this book will make the very difficult jobs of judges, lawyers, caseworkers, foster parents and anyone who is dealing with education issues for youth in the child welfare system, a little easier and their role in the process clearer.

—Kathleen M. McNaught

Acknowledgements

A huge thanks to Claire Sandt, not just for her skills as an editor, but for her incredible guidance, support, patience, and humor. This book would not have been possible without her talents.

To our terrific internal review team, including Mark Hardin, Mimi Laver, Jennifer Renne, Cecilia Fiermonte, Andrea Khoury, and Althea Izawa-Hayden, for all of their time and efforts to assist in making these materials the best they can be. Additional internal support was provided by Samia Noursi, Howard Davidson, Lisa Waxler, and Yvonne Brunot.

To a wonderful group of individuals who reviewed the various chapters of this book, provided valuable feedback and insight, including: Ann Barker, the Honorable Patricia Martin Bishop, the Honorable Constance Cohen, Sheryl Dicker, Judy Gerber, Leslie Heimlov, Lynn Katz, Nellis Kim, Miriam Krinsky, Katherine Locker, Leslie Said Margolis, the Honorable Juliette McKenna, Andrea Moore, and Debbie Winters.

Special thanks to Ron Palomares for contributing a piece to the book and for his thoughtful comments and insights provided from the school psychologist perspective.

Thanks to Center interns Lauren Onkeles, Adrianne Eckman, and Maya Bassford, for all of their research, proofing, cite checking and overall support.

Thanks to Emily Cooke, our federal project officer for the Resource Center on Legal and Judicial Issues for allowing this book to be possible.

Special thanks to my husband Bob, my family, and friends for their love and support throughout the writing of this book.

About this Book

This book is a tool for child welfare advocates to meet the education needs of children in foster care. A solid education can help these children transcend their circumstances and succeed in life. It should be a priority for all advocates in the child welfare system. Anyone in a position to advocate for children in foster care will benefit from this book. This includes judges, child welfare attorneys, foster and adoptive parents, biological parents, educators, and school staff.

Book at a Glance:

A glossary defines common education and child welfare terms that appear in this book.

Chapter 1 presents **general education advocacy strategies** all child welfare advocates should use in practice to improve educational outcomes for children in foster care.

Chapter 2 explains **education rights and key federal laws** advocates can use to leverage educational services and programs.

Chapter 3 demystifies the **special education process** and offers guidance on determining eligibility for special education services, creating a special education plan, and monitoring and implementing special education programming.

Chapter 4 focuses on the **education needs of young children**. An opportunity exists during the early childhood years to

intervene and get children on a healthy developmental path so they are ready to learn. This chapter explains how to access early childhood programs and services, including health care services, child care services, and services for children identified with a developmental delay or at risk of developmental delays.

Chapter 5 explains **how school discipline policies impact children in foster care**. It suggests ways advocates can work with schools to address the underlying issues a foster child presents that could lead to discipline. It offers tips for ensuring fair discipline and avoiding long-term harmful effects on academic success.

Chapter 6 shares **creative approaches to address education barriers for children in foster care** in four areas: direct advocacy, courtroom advocacy, legislative advocacy, and interagency collaboration.

You'll also find:

- At-a-glance practice tips to guide your education advocacy
- Special education process roadmap
- Tips from the bench for effective education advocacy
- An inside look at the role of foster parents as education decision makers
- Key IDEA regulations at your fingertips
- Education advocacy resources: websites, books, videos
- Common psychological tests used to evaluate children's education needs.

Glossary

Child welfare advocates should be familiar with the following education advocacy terms. They appear routinely throughout this book.

1. Attention deficit hyperactivity disorder (ADHD):

A condition that becomes apparent in some children in the preschool and early school years. The principal characteristics of ADHD are inattention, hyperactivity, and impulsivity. Because many children may have these symptoms, but at a low level, or the symptoms may be caused by another disorder, it is important that the child receive a thorough examination and appropriate diagnosis by a well-qualified professional.

2. Behavioral intervention plan (BIP):

Part of a comprehensive plan created by a child's IEP team that addresses a child's behavior caused by his or her disability. It generally includes regular or alternative disciplinary measures (i.e., loss of privileges), resulting from particular infractions of school rules, along with positive behavior intervention strategies and supports, as a part of a comprehensive plan to address the child's behavior.

3. Free and appropriate public education (FAPE):

Special education and related services provided at public expense, under public supervision and direction, and without charge. A FAPE must meet the standards of the state educational agency and include an appropriate preschool, elementary, or secondary school education in the state involved.

4. Child and family services review (CFSR):

CFSR is a comprehensive federal-state study of each state's performance in child abuse and neglect cases. It examines the performance of the entire state, including the child welfare agency, the courts, and other key agencies. A large team conducts the CFSR, including people from the federal government and people from the state —including consultants selected by the federal government and by the state. The CFSR uses multiple sources and types of information, including: statewide statistics; summaries of the state laws, regulations, rules and policies; intensive file reviews; and interviews of a variety of persons and groups who deal with the child welfare agency, including legal system representatives. There are several key stages of the CFSR: planning stage; statewide assessment; onsite review; issuance of the Final Report; and creation, implementation, and review of the Program Improvement Plan (PIP).

5. Early intervention services (EIS):

Developmental services provided under public supervision designed to meet the developmental needs of an infant or toddler with a physical, cognitive, communication, social, or adaptive disability. Services include:

- Family training, counseling, and home visits, special instruction, speech-language pathology and audiology services, occupational therapy, physical therapy, psychological services, service coordination services, medical services only for diagnostic or evaluation purposes, early identification, screening, and assessment services, health services necessary to enable the infant or toddler to benefit from the other; social work services, vision services, assistive technology devices and assistive technology services, and transportation and related costs that are necessary to enable an infant or toddler and the infant's or toddler's family to receive another service described in this paragraph.

- EIS are provided by qualified personnel. Services are provided at no cost except where federal or state law provides for a system of payments by families, including a schedule of sliding fees. 20 U.S.C. § 1432(4)

6. Extended school year (ESY):

Special education and related services provided to a child eligible under IDEA beyond the normal school year. The public agency provides services according to the child's IEP at no cost to the parents of the child. The services must meet the educational standards of the state. 34 C.F.R. § 300.309 (b) Extended school year services

7. Functional behavioral assessment (FBA):

A required assessment under IDEA that identifies problem behaviors (as well as the environmental factors and surrounding events that contribute to those behaviors) and identify appropriate interventions to teach more appropriate behaviors. FBAs must be conducted, at a minimum, when a child is disciplined by removal from school for over 10 days (or 10 days cumulative if the removals constitute a pattern), but can be used prior to such disciplinary action if determined by the IEP team to be appropriate.

8. Independent education evaluation (IEE):

A subsequent evaluation conducted at public expense by a qualified examiner who is not employed by the public agency responsible for the education of the child in question, when the parent disagrees with the prior evaluation obtained by the public agency. If the public agency wishes to refuse the request for a subsequent evaluation, it must obtain a favorable ruling through a due process hearing.

9. Individualized education program (IEP):

A written plan for each child with a disability eligible under IDEA that includes:

(1) a statement of the child's present levels of educational performance;

(2) a statement of measurable annual goals, including benchmarks or short-term objectives;

(3) a statement of the special education and related services and supplementary aids and services to be provided to the child, or on behalf of the child, and a statement of the program modifications or supports for school personnel that will be provided for the child;

(4) an explanation of the extent to which the child will not participate with non-disabled children in the regular class and activities;

(5) a statement of any individual modifications in the administration of State or district-wide assessments of student achievement that are needed in order for the child to participate in such assessment;

(6) the projected date for the beginning of the services and modifications, and the anticipated frequency, location, and duration of those services and modifications;

(7) a statement of needed transition services for the child;

(8) a statement of how the child's progress toward the annual goals will be measured and how the child's parents will be regularly informed about the child's progress. 20 U.S.C. § 1414 (d)

10. Individualized family service plan (IFSP):

Is a written plan containing—

(1) a statement of the infant's or toddler's present levels of development based on objective criteria;

(2) a statement of the family's resources, priorities, and concerns relating to enhancing the development of the family's infant or toddler with a disability;

(3) a statement of the major goals expected to be achieved for the infant or toddler and the family

(4) a statement of specific early intervention services necessary to meet the unique needs of the infant or toddler and the family

(5) a statement of the natural environments in which early intervention services shall appropriately be provided

(6) the projected dates for initiation of services and the anticipated duration of the services;

(7) the identification of the service coordinator from the profession most immediately relevant to the infant's or toddler's or family's needs (or who is otherwise qualified to carry out all applicable responsibilities under this subchapter) who will be responsible for the implementation of the plan and coordination with other agencies and persons; and

(8) the steps to be taken to support the transition of the toddler with a disability to preschool or other appropriate services. 20 U.S.C. § 1436 (d)

11. Interim alternative education setting (IAES):

A school setting, approved by a student's IEP team as an alternative to the current school setting, for a period of not more than 45 days, where the student can continue to participate in the general curriculum and continue to receive all of the services and modifications provided in the student's IEP to make progress toward their IEP goals. An IAES can be used for students who have been subject to discipline for weapon or drug related offenses, or who have been determined by a hearing officer to be a danger to themselves or others.

12. Least restrictive environment (LRE):

Children with disabilities eligible under IDEA must be educated with children who are not disabled to the maximum extent appropriate. Children with disabilities should only be placed in special classes, or separate schools, when the nature or severity of the disability of a child is such that education in regular classes with the use of supplementary aids and services cannot be achieved satisfactorily.

13. Manifestation hearing:

A meeting of the IEP team for a child with a disability eligible under IDEA, or suspected of eligibility under IDEA, when the child engages in behavior that is against the school rules and is at risk of suspension for 10 days or more. The team must decide, among other things, whether the child's actions were a manifestation of his or her disability.

14. Related service:

Services available under IDEA to be written into a child's IEP, including: transportation, and such developmental, corrective, and other supportive services as may be required to assist a child with a disability to benefit from special education.

15. Statement of transition services (sometimes known as individual transition plan):

A written statement included in a child's IEP when 14-years-old and older. It outlines a coordinated set of activities which promote movement from school to post-school activities, including post-secondary education, vocational training, integrated employment (including supported employment), continuing and adult education, adult services, independent living, or community participation. The statement of transition services is based upon the individual student's needs, taking into account the student's preferences and interests; and includes instruction, related services, community experiences, the development of employment and other post-school adult living objectives, and, when appropriate, daily living skills and functional vocational evaluation.

16. Surrogate parent:

A surrogate parent is an individual who stands in the shoes of a parent and makes educational decisions related to a child's eligibility under IDEA. A surrogate may be appointed by the state when no parent can be identified, the public agency, after reasonable efforts, cannot discover the whereabouts of a parent, or the child is a ward of the state under the laws of that state. A surrogate parent may represent the child in all matters relating to the identification, evaluation, and educational placement of the child; and the provision of FAPE to the child.

KEY EDUCATION ISSUES AND ROLES

INTRODUCTION

Do you have time in your schedule to focus on education issues? Aren't school systems responsible for educating ALL children, including those in foster care? With so much on your plate, can't you leave this to the school system and others to address?

Of course not. Sure, local school systems should do their part, but you as child welfare professionals need to start focusing on and prioritizing the education needs of children in care. Schools cannot be expected to address the needs of children in our system without input and advocacy from you. You should also ensure that child welfare systems, in addition to school systems, are doing all they can to meet these children's education needs.

How? Whether you are a judge; attorney for the child, parent or child welfare agency; a social worker; parent; or foster parent, you each have reasons why a child's education needs should be a top concern. This chapter outlines your role in achieving better education outcomes for children in foster care.

WHY CARE ABOUT EDUCATION?

Children in foster care, perhaps more than other students, need a solid education to help ensure a successful future. A 2002 national study of children in the child welfare system reveals 27% of 6- to-17 year olds have a high level of emotional or behavioral problems.[1] The study also found that 28% of the children living with relatives and foster parents have a physical, learning, or mental health condition that limits their activities.[2] Another study shows that abuse and neglect represent a significant risk factor for poor academic performance and grade repetition.[3] That study shows maltreated students are 2.5 times more likely to repeat a grade than nonmaltreated students.[4]

Studies show that youth in foster care with unmet education needs are at higher risk for homelessness, poverty, public assistance, and juvenile or adult court involvement.[5] In contrast, one study shows that when school programs focus on education needs of children in care, the results are improved educational performance, decreased maladaptive behavior, and lower drop-out rates, all of which aid successful transitions to employment or higher education.[6]

In line with these findings, the federal government has made the education needs of children in care a priority for the child welfare system. The Adoption and Safe Families Act (ASFA) federal regulations, effective March 2000, require states to undergo child and family service reviews (CFSRs).[7] These federal reviews examine seven general outcomes related to children's safety, permanency and well-being to determine a state's overall performance in child protection cases. One well-being outcome is whether "children receive appropriate services to meet their educa-tional needs."[8] States risk losing federal funds if they are not achieving these outcomes, including meeting the education needs of children in care.

In addition, addressing education needs can help achieve permanency for children in foster care. Youth who are on track educationally, attending school regularly, and not having behavior problems at school can be easier to find permanent family resources than youth who are having multiple school problems.

HOW TO MEET THE EDUCATION NEEDS OF CHILDREN IN CARE

What can you do to make sure the education needs of children in foster care are met? The following steps will get you started. Future chapters explore some of these issues in more detail.

Secure and Maintain Accurate and Accessible School Records

For children to achieve academic success, courts, attorneys, caseworkers, foster parents, and other advocates in the child welfare system must have access to accurate school records for all students in foster care. Records not produced in a timely manner will hinder a smooth transition to a new school. Incomplete, inaccurate, or lost records prevent appropriate school placements.

Child welfare agency and school system records have confidentiality protections attached. Schools and agencies must protect the confidentiality rights of the child and parents. Therefore, the easiest way for the child welfare system to gain access to a child's records is with parental consent (see sidebar #2). Generally, federal law requires that student records are kept confidential, unless a parent agrees to release the information.[9] If a parent does not consent to the release of education information, child and agency attorneys, and judges, can pursue other legal avenues to obtain this information. These include determining who is the legal "parent" under federal and state law, and reviewing the exceptions to parental consent such as seeking a court order or subpoena if a viable legal argument can be made for accessing the records.[10] (See chapter 2 for more information on legal confidentiality requirements.)

Once access to the education records is established, there is still work for you to do. Federal law requires the child welfare agency to include a child's education records "to the extent available and accessible" as part of its case plan.[11] Often the educational histories for these children are key to determining future school programming for the child. Agency attorneys need to see that these records are in the case files, and remind the caseworkers of their duty to obtain these records. In addition, federal law requires that education records be shared with the foster care provider.[12]

While federal law requires agencies to have a child's education records, there is no such requirement for children's attorneys and advocates. In an ideal world, all child advocates would have and review complete education records for their clients. The American Bar Association has issued standards for attorneys who represent children, suggesting that reviewing school records may be required for a thorough and independent investigation in a child welfare case (see sidebar #3).[13] Ultimately, the amount of effort needed to pursue education information must be determined on a case-by-case basis, and

be prioritized for those clients where there is a need or lack of information (See sidebar #4).

Judges can ask parties to produce relevant documents for the court. Judges may need to see documents such as report cards and education evaluations, to ensure efforts are in place to protect the child's well-being at each child welfare hearing. (See sidebar #5 for more creative steps judges can take.)

Practitioners' Roles:

- **All advocates:** Ensure access to education records by obtaining consent of the parent, determining who is the legal parent under the law, or seeking a court order for access.
- **Child welfare agencies:** Include education records as part of your case plan, and share education records with foster care providers.

Communicate with the School System

Accessing and reviewing records is the first step. Unless school and child welfare professionals work together, and understand the impact collaboration can have on children, we cannot expect improvements. This involves communication between the systems on two levels:

Systemwide communication. It is essential that the school system, child welfare agency, and court communicate regularly. One way to foster communication is to designate a staff member to serve as a liaison to the school system from both the child welfare agency and the court system. Designated staff not only should be the point people when education issues arise, but they should also initiate systemic reform, and educate school administrators and staff about the foster care system and the issues these children face. Schools must first know about the unique needs of youth in foster care before they can be expected to aid these children. (More detailed examples of systemic collaboration can be found in chapter 6.)

Case-specific communication. Children's attorneys, parents' attorneys, and agency attorneys (in coordination with caseworkers and/or foster parents) can introduce themselves and talk to a child's teachers, guidance counselor, or other school staff. Such communications may depend on the parents' consent or the agency's authority to make education decisions (see sidebars #1 and #2). If legal arguments support disclosure, courts can create clear written orders authorizing schools to communicate with various individuals on behalf of a child.

Practitioners' Roles:

- **Child welfare agencies:** Consistently communicate with the school as part of your casework responsibilities.
- **Child advocates:** Communicate with the school to the extent necessary to represent your client effectively (see sidebar #4).
- **Parents, and their attorneys:** Retain the right to communicate with the school until parental rights are terminated or another court order or state law restricts your right to do so (see sidebar #1).
- **Judges:** Use your judicial authority to obtain important information about a child promptly. Use your court education liaison, if one exists, to obtain educational information.

Continue Prior School Placements When Feasible

Despite histories of abuse and neglect, many children in foster care have had positive school experiences. School may be the only stable environment these children have known. When a child is removed from home, separated from parents and sometimes siblings, the child's world is turned upside down. As long as the current school placement is appropriate, and the child can receive necessary services in that school setting, every effort needs to be made to minimize disruptions in the child's education. Statistics show that school mobility correlates with school difficulties. One study shows that by fourth grade, mobile students are an average of four months behind their more stable classmates on standardized tests, and by sixth grade they are as much as a year behind.[14]

At times the goal of school stability may be inconsistent with the goal of permanency in a child's living arrangement. However, the point is that advocates should be aware of the damaging effects changing schools can have on a child's education. It may be a reality in your jurisdiction that a child will have to change schools when entering foster care, but child welfare professionals should take all steps to avoid a school change when possible. Advocates must analyze the pros and cons of any prospective placement for a child in foster care. Part of that analysis must consider the educational impact on the child of any proposed change. (See sidebar #5 for more discussion of this issue.)

However, there will be times when advocates may favor a school move. For

Sidebar 1

Who is the Education Decision Maker?

Determining the education decision maker for a child in foster care is critical for educational success. Yet who decides is not clear in law and practice.

When a child enters foster care, caseworkers typically assume responsibility for enrolling the child in school. However, absent a specific state statute or court order authorizing the agency to make education decisions on the child's behalf, the parent(s) needs to be involved in every step of the process. If there is a question at any point in the case as to the parents' availability, willingness, or ability to make important education decisions, consult state statutes to see if they clarify this issue in your jurisdiction. An agency or child's attorney may need to seek a court order clarifying who is authorized to make education decisions on behalf of the child, or specifying that the court itself wants that role.

If the child has a disability, and qualifies under the Individuals with Disabilities Education Act (IDEA), a surrogate parent may need to be appointed as the decision maker. (See chapter 3 for detailed analysis of education decision making authority under IDEA).

example, parents may object to placement with a relative who lives within the original school's jurisdiction. This objection may outweigh the interest in keeping the child in the same school. Parents' advocates must counsel parents about the importance of decisions that are in the best interest of the child and their effect on reunification. Ultimately, they must advocate the parent's position to the court.

Child advocates or attorneys, acting in the child's best interest or for their expressed wishes, also may not be able to support a living arrangement that would keep school placement stable. For example, a child may prefer to live with a relative in another town or state, or the local placement may not be in the child's best interest.

Practitioners' Roles:

- **All advocates:** If removal from the parents is necessary, all advocates should ensure efforts have been made to place the child with a relative or foster home that enables the child to remain in his or her current school.
- **Child welfare agencies:** Make efforts to locate relatives or access foster homes within the child's school district, or arrange with the school and the proposed placement for the child to stay enrolled even if placed outside the school's jurisdiction.
- **Agency attorneys:** Ask caseworkers about these efforts in all cases where the agency is advocating a move for the child.

Rationale for Parent Attorney Cooperation

There are many reasons why attorneys for parents, and their clients, should consider cooperating with the agency, courts, and/or child's attorney in education matters, regardless of whether the parents consented to the child's entry into foster care or were court ordered to relinquish the child.

Reasons supporting parent cooperation:
- shows the parent's concern about their child's education
- ensures current caregivers have full knowledge of their child's educational history
- ensures continued appropriate academic programming for their child
- aids their reunification case

Reasons why parents may not want to cooperate include:
- believe they can continue to make appropriate decisions and monitor the child's educational progress without agency or court assistance
- believe the agency, foster parent, and/or court CANNOT make appropriate decisions and monitor child's educational progress
- embarrassed about child welfare involvement (doesn't want school to know)
- angry at courts, agency, or others
- unable to see damage that failure to cooperate may do to child's education

Parents' attorneys need to discuss these reasons with their clients, counsel them on the effects the decision will have on their children, and ultimately on their case.

- **Child advocates and parent attorneys:** Work with your clients to identify relatives or other placement resources. Argue to the court against moving a child because of the negative impact on the child's education.
- **Judges:** Ask about efforts to keep a child in a school placement each time a party advocates for a child to be moved. Weigh the negative impact of a change in school placement when deciding whether to allow a placement move for a child.

Get Young Children into School Programs

When thinking about school services, don't forget preschoolers. Statistics show that 40% of all children entering foster care are less than five years old.[15] Early interventions may be the key to future school success for younger children experiencing, or at risk of experiencing, developmental delays. A recent study released by the U.S. Department of Health and Human Services highlights the success of Early Head Start (a federal early intervention program for children from birth through age three). The national study reveals that children completing Early Head Start achieve gains on standardized tests of cognitive and language development. The study also shows that such children may need fewer special learning interventions in the future, and perform better on critical social-emotional tasks, such as relating to their parents, paying attention, and behaving appropriately.[16] Young children in foster care must be identified and assessed early to determine needs and eligibility for services and programs, such as Early and Periodic Screening, Diagnosis, and Treatment (EPSDT), Head Start, early intervention services under the Individuals with Disabilities Education Act (IDEA), and others.[17]

Practitioners' Roles:

- **Child welfare agencies, child advocates, and parents' attorneys:** Identify public and private education programs in the community that serve young children. Push for early identification, thorough assessments, and appropriate services and program placements.
- **Attorneys for parents and children:** Oversee the child welfare agency and ensure proper referrals and applications are made.
- **Agency attorneys:** Work with caseworkers and foster parents to ensure services are being arranged for these young children. Seek court orders to ensure timely evaluation and services for the child.
- **Judges:** Ask about information related to healthy development for young children (e.g., whether developmental and mental health screenings have been completed and whether enrollments in early childhood programs have been arranged).

Keep Older Children in School

Disrupting education programming can be devastating to older children, and can lead to school failure. Research shows that changing schools during high school diminishes the chances for graduation.[18] Another study shows that teens in foster care are less likely to be in college preparatory classes in high school, even when they have similar test scores and grades as nonfoster youth.[19]

School moves can be especially difficult, causing loss of credits and affecting graduation status. Foster children are often behind because of prior home life difficulties. They may give up hope of a high school diploma if they are pushed further behind because of curriculum differences between their original school and their new placement.

Attorneys and judges need to encourage teenage students to remain in school, complete their educations, and pursue higher education goals. It is important to mentor and counsel youth, and always assume that a conversation about continued education is needed. Higher education avenues may be college or vocational and technical training. Find out what avenues are available and appropriate and discuss them with the children with whom you work. Be sure to explore financial assistance programs available for foster youth. For example, some states provide foster children a free or reduced tuition for in-state higher education or technical training.[20]

Standards of Representation for Children's Attorneys: Education Issues

Under the CAPTA Reauthorization of 2003, attorneys representing children in abuse and neglect cases are required to undergo training before their first case. This training should include, among other things, information related to education. The ABA's Standards of Practice for Lawyers Who Represent Children in Abuse and Neglect Cases give guidance to children's attorneys regarding their duties when representing their clients. Standards relating to education are excerpted below:*

- B-1 and Commentary: Child's attorney should identify appropriate professional resources (this contemplates that the attorney will identify educational services for which the child will qualify under law and teachers with whom the child feels it is important to maintain contact).

- C-1 Commentary: Child's attorney should meet with the child when the child has received a school suspension or other similar changes.

- C-2: Child's attorney should conduct thorough, continuing, and independent investigations, which may include:
  (1): reviewing school records,
  (5): obtaining necessary authorizations for the release of information,
  (6): interviewing individuals involved with the child, including school personnel,
  (8): Attending treatment, placement, administrative hearings, other proceedings involving legal issues, and school case conferences or staffings concerning the child. (The child's attorney should attend to present the child's perspective at such meetings, even if courts will not compensate the attorney for these collateral meetings. Child's attorney may not need to attend if another person, such as a caseworker, can get information or present the child's perspective).

- C-4: Child's attorney should seek appropriate services (by court order if necessary) to access entitlements, to protect the child's interests and to implement a service plan, including educational services.

- C-5: Child's attorney should assure that a child with special needs receives appropriate services to address the physical, mental, or developmental disabilities, which may include special education and related services.

- D-12: Child's attorney may request authority for the court to pursue issues on behalf of the child, administratively or judicially, even if those issues do no specifically arise from the court appointment. For example school/education issues, especially for a child with disabilities.

Sidebar 3 continued

- **H-3:** The court should enter an order authorizing lawyer access to the child and all privileged information regarding the child, including school records.

- **I-2:** The court should provide educational programs on the role of the child's attorney, including training on child development, needs, and abilities, and information on accessible educational resources for child clients.

*Consult the standards for complete language (available at http://www.abanet.org/child/childrep.html)

Practitioners' Roles:

- **Agency caseworkers and attorneys:** Become familiar with the program and financial support community options available in the community and present these options to teens in foster care.
- **Child advocates:** Become familiar with financial support programs and discuss the options with clients to ensure they are making thoughtful decisions about their futures.
- **Parents:** If you still have positive relationships with your children, even though they are in foster care, play a role by encouraging continued education.
- **Parents' attorneys:** Give parent clients information about community resources as well, both for their own adult education goals as well as to help support their child's goals.
- **Judges:** Help youth think about their futures. Some encouraging words from the bench may impact the future of a vulnerable teenager who needs adult support and guidance.

Ensure All Children in Care Get Good School Services and Placements

Often we hear about special school services only in the context of special education. However, good school systems provide special services to all students. It is part of a school's basic curriculum, and good teachers and guidance counselors will assist children with difficult issues, regardless of whether they have an identified disability. Many regular education students need to take advantage of these extra services to achieve academic success. Although children in foster care do not have a special legal entitlement to these services, they can benefit tremendously from them. For example, some schools offer special counseling groups formed by the guidance counselor's office, afterschool enrichment programs, or special classes during the day focusing on things like organization or self esteem.

Children in care often need this extra help to keep them on par with their peers. However, too often services provided by the school system are the first to be

Deciding What Actions to Take in Education Matters:
Tips for Child Advocates

Child advocates need to determine to what extent they must get involved with education matters on a case-by-case basis. Here are some tips:

- Start by communicating with the child, caseworker, and foster parents in the case.

- Ask about education issues, such as school attendance, grades, teacher and progress reports, discipline referrals, and the client's attitude toward school.

- Watch for an alarming LACK of information about the child's education. For example, a client appears sullen and depressed, says she gets no services in school, is failing almost all her classes, and the caseworker and foster parent have no information about school performance.

- In cases where education needs are obvious but no one has pursued evaluations or services for the child, the child advocate should be the catalyst for action.

- Some cases will not need significant intervention, but may need basic investigation to confirm a child is doing well in school. For example, a child that tells the advocate he likes school, the foster parent reports that the child gets good grades, and the caseworker says she is regularly in touch with the teacher and receives all good reports, may indicate the child advocate does not need to intervene. This does not mean an advocate should not confirm this information with a quick call to the school or by obtaining some basic school records.

- For situations requiring action, advocates may need to independently seek educational records, communicate with the school, determine if services and the placement are appropriate for the child, and attend meetings or school hearings with the child. The situation may require anything from a few phone calls to multiple, lengthy meetings and hearings.

eliminated due to budgetary constraints. School-related services for children in care can also come from sources outside the school system. The child welfare agency can provide school-type services, such as private in-home tutoring, mentoring groups, or summer programs. If more of these services were available to children in foster care, fewer children might be identified as needing special education services or having other education difficulties.

Practitioners' Roles:

- **All advocates:** Become familiar with services available in schools and make efforts to get and keep these services in place for children in care. In addition to advocating for the school system to supply all the supports it can, make sure the child welfare system provides other needed services.
- **Child welfare agencies:** Focus on what programs the schools lack, and find or establish new programs in the community to fill gaps.
- **Judges:** Order the child welfare agency to provide specific services for children (e.g., tutoring or mentoring) if they are warranted in a child welfare case.
- **Attorneys for children and parents:** Advocate and seek court orders for services to ensure agency action and/or follow through.

Obtain Special Education Services and Placements for Children Who Qualify

Two federal laws govern special services for children with unique education needs: the Individuals with Disabilities Education Act and Section 504 of the Rehabilitation Act (Section 504).[21] These laws, detailed in other chapters, make special provisions for students with disabilities to ensure they can access a free and appropriate public education (FAPE).

Special education services and placements under IDEA are vital to foster children with disabilities. Learning, physical, and emotional disabilities, among others, can prevent a student from succeeding in school, especially when left unaddressed. Unfortunately, the initial identification of need is often missed, and the child struggles in a regular education classroom for months or even years, falling further and further behind. Or, children in care may be identified as disabled, but the right services are not identified and/or provided by the school. Finally, getting appropriate special education placements can be difficult.

On the flip side, overidentifying foster children as special education students can be a problem. Many children in care who do not meet the special education criteria are identified as special education students. Some schools are quick to label a foster child as a special education student, hoping to remove that troubled student from the general population. The IDEA can truly serve children in foster care only when the right students (those with disabilities that impact their educations) are provided the right services in the right placements.

Practitioners' Roles:

- **Attorneys for all parties:** Advocate for the child's education needs within the child welfare case. Ask judges to order assessments, which will be used to speed the school identification process.
- **Attorneys and social workers:** Supply the school with documentation, such as confirmation of physical and mental health diagnosis.

Helping Children in Foster Care "Reach for the Stars": An Interview with Judge Constance Cohen, Des Moines, Iowa

Q: How long have you been a juvenile court judge? What did you do before you became a judge?

A: I have been a juvenile court judge for nine years. Teaching was my first career; I did that for 12 years. I am also a mom of two. I left teaching to go to law school when my children were four and six years old. I had found that between working and raising children I was teaching 24/7, and that was too much. I have the greatest admiration for teachers, especially at the elementary level. I also experienced frustration as a teacher and at times felt powerless to get children the help they needed.

I remember a case while I was teaching where the student needed to be placed in a facility that could provide psychiatric care. The entire school team agreed that this was necessary, but then, at the last minute, the parents changed their minds. I remember thinking that if I were a lawyer I would have more power to do what was best for the child. Attorneys really have an opportunity to do so much for children. So, I went to law school.

Q: When did you first start addressing educational needs as part of your role as juvenile judge?

A: I have asked how children who come before me in court are doing in school from the very beginning. I think that how a child is doing in school is the greatest barometer of how a child is doing in life. After being on the bench a few months I developed my signature line: "You have the bad luck to have a judge who used to be a teacher." I always ask about grades, behavior, and educational needs.

I always think back to when I was teaching fourth grade. One of my students was having trouble focusing one day. The student confided to me that the night before she had seen her mother stabbed by her stepfather while she hid behind the couch. She was able to tell me about that because I had been her teacher and she trusted me. I now think, what if she had been taken away from her home (and school) that night; from everyone she knew and trusted and could talk to? If that child had to go to a different school I shudder to think what would have happened to her. As a result of my memory of this student, I began to ask the attorneys and caseworkers in my courtroom if moving the child into foster care would disrupt school placement. I ask these questions even in ex-parte temporary removal requests.

Q: What do you see as your role in assisting a child within the juvenile court system to have his or her special education needs met?

A: I see my court as a court of last resort for many of these children. If education needs are still not being addressed by the time the child ends up in my court-room, there are big problems. If I don't ask, who will? Why put together a beautiful home on a crumbling foundation? Education is a necessary piece for success for children. When I train judges and lawyers, I talk with them about what the issues were when they were in school. For many of us our biggest problem was if our hair frizzed on the day of cheerleading tryouts or what our friends would think of our new outfit; these children have serious issues. We need to make sure they aren't being dropped at the front door and running out the back. We need to know their special needs are identified and addressed.

Q: Has your involvement in education issues changed over the years? If so, how?

A: Over time, I have learned a great deal more about the issues. I have benefited from Judge Leonard Edward's school of judicial leadership. He was instrumental in drafting the California court rules that specify what judges should ask regarding educational stability. As a result, over the years I have gotten more aggressive about education. Attorneys and workers know that they must be prepared to answer questions about the child's education when they come before me in my courtroom. I don't just ask questions. I know what an IEP is; I know what FERPA and IDEA say; and folks know I know. I have spent a lot of time dealing with education issues and making specific orders about them.

Sometimes it can be frustrating, because there are things about school district policy that I cannot change. But that can be an opportunity to get creative and think outside of the box. For example, if there is a delay in having a child placed in a new school, I have been known to order a child to read two books a week and to provide me with book reports. That way, I at least know the child is keeping up with his reading and writing skills while he is waiting for his new school placement.

Another change I have made recently is I have gone to a different level of inquiry for the older youth. I have had many kids come back and say that they feel they were shortchanged by getting a GED instead of a high school diploma. So now when the recommendation for an older teen is to get their GED, I will question that recommendation. That is not to say that sometimes getting a GED is an appropriate goal; but sometimes it is the easy way out. I like to question whether this is the star this child should be reaching for, or if they have the ability to reach for another star. For example, our jurisdiction has recently had an increase in our Bosnian population. I have seen these children struggle with the English language, as it is so different from their native language. However, if I see a child who is speaking flawless English after two or three years, and the recommendation is for that child to get a GED, I am going to look long and hard at that. If he could learn a new language in two or three years he must be very bright. Should the goal for that child really be a GED?

Q: How do you get information about the child's education, and what kinds of education information do you think is important to your decision making?

A: Information about how a child is doing in school often shows up in reports before I ask. I will put in my court orders "Agency shall bring school records to next court hearing." In almost every case involving school-age children, I will see the school records. Older children will often bring their own report cards to court, or give them to their lawyers or juvenile court workers; sometimes the information is folded into the report.

When children are in special education I always want to see their IEPs or IFSPs for the young children. I also see a strong need to order appropriate evaluations for these children. Most judges order fundamental evaluations such as hearing, dental, medical, and eye exams. What judges need to do is think about the totality of the child's well-being. In addition to ordering the evaluations, Judges also need to ensure the child welfare system has access to existing evaluations. Judges need to familiarize themselves with statutes regarding sharing of information. They need to familiarize themselves with FERPA, and understand that they have the ability to order records released under FERPA exceptions. Judges need to start bringing people to the table and discuss where, if any, missing links exist. For example, our child welfare agency got a grant for a computer data system that will help share information among systems—including education.

Besides written records, I get information from the parties involved in the child welfare case. I am vigilant that all children's cases are staffed regularly, and I have ordered people to go to staffings. I have certain attorneys I know are knowledgeable about education issues and will appoint cases to them. I have been known to order a GAL to talk with a child's teacher.

Another way I have gotten information about a child's education is by ordering school personnel to come to hearings. I recently issued an order for the principal or a designee to appear at the next hearing for a child to supply information and explain why the child's needs were not being met.

I am also a strong proponent of using family group conferencing to obtain educational information and to determine what is best for a child. It is truly amazing what relatives and others are willing to do to help a child succeed. For example, family group conferencing could result in an aunt coming forward and being willing to drive a child every day across county lines to be sure the child completes the year in her home school. That is true dedication, but the effort is invaluable to that child's education.

The biggest job that needs to be done is to get child welfare judges and professionals to overcome the myth that they can't access educational information. Judges and lawyers need to understand that they can have access. Good checklists exist to help cue judges about which issues they should be asking. Beg, borrow, or steal materials from other judges or other jurisdictions if you need to. Judges need to be willing to use these checklists and other tools and then go another step further if needed. Judges in these cases need to be more than just receptacles; they need to be activists.

Q: What training should judges and others have in this area?

A: The National Council of Juvenile and Family Court Judges (NCJFCJ) has created opportunities for learning more about how judges can impact education outcomes. At the recent Child Abuse and Neglect Institute at the NCJFCJ weeklong training, a session on meeting educational needs was included for the first time. Judges need to understand basic child development, IDEA, FERPA, and Chafee. Iowa has a new law that provides transition teams for children in the foster care system who are 15? and older. These children need to know that there are entitlements out there that can assist them with college expenses. I have ordered the Department to pursue Chafee money for a particular child.

Additionally, I recently took part in a statewide training on education needs of young children. Many people don't know about IDEA Part C services that are available for young children. Judge Cindy Lederman (Miami, FL) and folks from Zero to Three came and provided valuable information to the judges in my state. It is really a priority for the child welfare system to ask about the health and development of these young children as early as possible. In Iowa we are plagued with methamphetamine, crack cocaine, and marijuana problems. We are also blessed with a child protection center that is led by Dr. Shah who is an incredible, internationally acclaimed pediatrician, and has expertise in drug-exposed children. It can make such a big difference if we catch health and developmental issues early. Judges should also know that there is a wonderful young children's checklist entitled "Checklist for Healthy Development of Foster Children" developed by the Permanent Judicial Commission on Justice for Children in New York (and available on their website at http://www.courts.state.ny.us/pjcjc/). This document lists key questions to ask when dealing with young children. There is an abridged version that only has two questions about education. At a minimum shouldn't all judges be asking at least those two questions?

In addition to training for our judges, we also get involved with training for other child welfare professionals in our community. Through the model court project, we have had brown bag lunches offering free education training for juvenile court attorneys, workers, and staff.

Q: What limits your ability to focus on education needs?

A: Our heavy judicial caseloads limit our ability to be as involved in each case as we would like. I am very dedicated to the one-judge, one-court model, but with 1000 cases it is hard to give each case the attention and follow up needed. And with those caseloads it is hard to do the other proactive things that make the system work smoother, for example collaborating with other people and agencies.

Another limitation is the walls, built up over time, that make it difficult for different systems to work together. It is important that we break down these walls. When I first got on the bench, the court and the agency were very disjointed and distrustful of other agencies and people. We have to get over that by sitting down with people and finding common ground. We have the technology to do so much in the way of collaboration. A great example of good use of technology is the E-PASS system that exists in California. It gives multiple entities access to a child's education records, immunization history, etc. These systems save money in the long run. For example, if we didn't have a three-week delay waiting on records to get a child back into a school, we wouldn't be losing the per-diem dollars that the Department of Education pays to local school districts based on attendance.

Q: What advice do you have for new juvenile court judges about educational needs in dependency cases?

A: Ask an old veteran who to talk with to get several different perspectives. Meet educators who can provide answers. Find information about FERPA and other education laws. Know key school people; there is no time better than your early days on the bench to go out and make these contacts and begin these conversations and relationships, especially because they do not yet have any preconceived notions about you. There is no better time to extend yourself, before you are inundated with cases. Talk with teachers and ask them what questions you should be asking. Visit schools—elementary, state training schools, etc. Find out what they have to offer. Have a phone number of someone in your community to bounce ideas off of. Figure out the right questions. Strongly urge a one-family one-judge system so you can establish relationships with the children that come before your court.

Judges also need to vigilantly review cases and think about the school year when setting cases. I will set cases for review in late September, even if that is sooner than six months since the last hearing, so I can know how the summer went and how the transition to school is going. This is to ensure the child is not too far into the school year so that issues can be addressed before too much damage is done.

- **Judges:** Resolve the issue of who has education decision-making authority so that issue will not delay school services.
- **Child welfare agencies:** Supply and train foster parents and others to be parent surrogates. This ensures that knowledgeable and suitable people are making decisions for children with disabilities in foster care. (See chapter 3 for more on appointing education surrogates.)
- **All advocates:** Get involved in the school system's process to ensure children in foster care are placed appropriately. Ensure that students who do not need restrictive placements are not being forced into these settings unnecessarily.

Ensure that Children in Foster Care are Fairly Disciplined in School

A recent national study found 32% of 12- to-17 year olds in the child welfare system have been suspended or expelled from school.[22] Another study determined that physically abused children had three times the number of discipline referrals as their nonmaltreated peers.[23] Children in foster care are frequently disciplined by schools for behaviors resulting from their abuse or neglect histories or from involvement in the child welfare system. Some examples of these behaviors are acting aggressively to protect themselves, being disruptive to seek attention, rejecting others to protect from being rejected themselves, lying to please others, or skipping school because of school phobias.

All children who are eligible for IDEA or Section 504 services, including children in care with these plans, are subject to different disciplinary procedures than regular education students. These procedures

determine if a relationship exists between the disability and the behavior that led to the discipline. If a relationship can be found, the school must provide additional or improved services to address that behavior, in lieu of punishment that keeps the child from accessing his education.

Consider a student who is diagnosed with Attention Deficit Hyperactivity Disorder (ADHD) and is receiving special education services. If this child is disciplined for finding a Swiss army knife at the bus stop and bringing it to school to show his friends, advocates might argue that the behavior of bringing the knife to school is directly related to the impulsivity found in children with ADHD.

These children need strong advocates to ensure their circumstances are considered before punishments are imposed. In today's "zero tolerance" school environment, this can be hard to do.

Practitioners' Roles:

- **All advocates:** Remember that all students have due process rights when subjected to certain disciplinary infractions. Become familiar with these due process rights and the school's disciplinary procedures, and advocate at disciplinary hearings and appeals if necessary. (See chapter 5 for more on due process protections when students are disciplined at school.)
- **Advocates, particularly attorneys:** Understand the complicated laws involving discipline of students eligible under IDEA and Section 504 and learn how to lead students with disabilities through the complex web of manifestation hearings, behavioral intervention plans (BIPs) and individualized education program (IEP) meetings to revise students' education plans.

CONCLUSION

The child welfare and education systems share responsibility for positive education outcomes for children in care. As an attorney, judge, or other child welfare advocate, you can play a key role ensuring these children's needs are met in the school system, and improve the chances of educational success by taking action within the child welfare system. When you understand what laws apply, what programs are available and how school processes work, you can look for creative solutions to problems and innovative ways to help educate children. These efforts can have a tremendous impact on the futures of children in foster care.

Endnotes

[1] Kortenkamp, Katherine & Jennifer Ehrle. *The Well-Being of Children Involved with the Child Welfare System: A National Overview.* (Series B, No. B-43) Washington, DC: The Urban Institute, January 2002, 2.

[2] Ibid. 3.

[3] Eckenrode, J., M. Laird & J. Doris. "School Performance and Disciplinary Problems Among Abused and Neglected Children." *Developmental Psychology* 29(1), 1993, 59.

[4] Ibid., 57.

[5] See discussion in Godsoe, C. "Caught Between Two Systems: How Exceptional Children in Out-of-Home Care Are Denied Equality in Education." *Yale Law and Policy Review* 19, 2000, 81-164.

[6] Ayasse, Robert H. "Addressing the Needs of Foster Children: The Foster Youth Services Program." *Social Work in Education* 17(4), 1995, 207-216.

[7] ASFA Regulations, 45 C.F.R. §1355.31 et seq.

[8] 45 C.F.R. §1355.34(b)(1)(iii)(B).

[9] 20 U.S.C. § 1232g; 34 C.F.R. § 99. This is a federal law, passed in 1974, commonly referred to as the Buckley Amendment.

[10] Regardless of whether agencies and child advocates are given access to the child's school records, parents continue to retain the right to access these records as well. The FERPA regulations spell out that the only way for the parent to lose this right would be if "the agency or institution has been pro-vided with evidence that there is a court order, state statute or legally binding document relating to such matters as divorce separation or custody that specifically revokes these rights." 34 C.F.R. § 99.4.

[11] Adoption Assistance and Child Welfare Act, 42 U.S.C. § 675(1)(C).

[12] Ibid.

[13] American Bar Association House of Delegates. *American Bar Association Standards of Practice for Lawyers Who Represent a Child in Abuse and Neglect Cases,* C-2. Washington, DC: American Bar Association, February 5, 1996, 9. See sidebar #3 for more details about the ABA Standards as they pertain to education issues.

[14] Jacobson, Linda. "Moving Targets." *Education Weekly.* April 4, 2001, 3.

[15] Dicker, Sheryl & Elysa Gordon. "Early Intervention and Early Childhood Programs: Essential Tools for Child Welfare Advocacy." *Clearinghouse Review, Journal of Poverty Law and Policy* 34 (11-12), March-April 2001, 727.

[16] Love, John M. et al.. "Making a Difference in the Lives of Infants and Toddlers and Their Families." U.S. Department of Health and Human Services, Administration for Children and Families, June 2002. Available at http://www.acf.hhs.gov/programs/core/ongoing_research/ehs/impacts_exesum/impacts_exesum.html#1.

[17] These federal programs are detailed in chapters 2 and 4.

[18] Juliennelle, Patricia. "The New McKinney-Vento Act: Promoting Student Achievement Through Educational Stability." *Children's Legal Rights Journal* 22(1), Spring 2002, 21 n.27 (citing Rumberger, Russel et al. "Policy Analysis for California Education, The Educational Consequences of Mobility for California Students and Schools." *PACE Policy Brief,* May 1999, 4).

[19] Blome, Wendy. "What Happens to Foster Kids: Educational Experiences of a Random Sample of Foster Care Youth and a Matched Group of Non-Foster Care Youth." *Child and Adolescent Social Work Journal* 14(1), February 1997.

[20] Maryland is one of a few states that allow reduced tuition for youth in foster care.

[21] Individuals with Disabilities Education Act, 20 U.S.C. §1400, et. seq.; Section 504 of the Rehabilitation Act, 29 U.S.C. § 794, et seq.

[22] Kortenkamp, 2002, 2.

[23] Eckenrode, 1993, 59.

EDUCATION LAW PRIMER

INTRODUCTION

Laws can be powerful tools to meet the education needs of children in foster care. Like any tools, if you don't know how to use them, they don't provide much help. This chapter addresses key laws relating to the right to education, school records and information, children with disabilities, school discipline and access to a quality education. It also examines laws relating to educating two special populations: young children and teenagers. Practice tips help child welfare advocates better serve the education needs of children and access school programs and services.

RIGHT TO EDUCATION
History
State laws create the right to a public education for children in this country.[1] All states require that children of certain ages attend school.[2] Most states' laws provide criminal sanctions for parents whose children do not regularly attend school.[3] From this requirement to attend school, children obtain the *right* to attend school, if they are within the required ages.[4]

Federal law applies to the education of children in two ways. First, most federal laws related to education attach financial incentives to encourage state compliance. States receive significant federal support in educating the children of their state if they comply with these laws. Second, federal law applies through the U.S. constitution. While the constitution does not require states to provide public education for children, it does require that if states create a right to public education, providing that education must not violate the constitution.[5]

Practice Tips:

- Ensure children in foster care receive the same right to an education as all children.
- Use the laws discussed in this article to benefit children in foster care in your state.
- Learn which laws have specific provisions for children in foster care.
- Be aware that problems affecting the general right to an education of a child in foster care often result from another factor in that child's life, other than the child's direct involvement in the child welfare system. For example:
  - Children born to non-U.S. citizens, or who are non-U.S. citizens themselves, have the same right to a public education as children who are citizens.[6]
- Some children lacking proper immunizations may not be allowed to enroll in school, although exceptions exist.[7]
- Teenage girls who become pregnant before completing high school cannot be segregated in special programs, nor can they be excluded from school entirely.[8]

SCHOOL RECORDS AND INFORMATION
Family Educational Rights and Privacy Act (FERPA)
Passed in 1974, this federal law protects the privacy interests of parents and students regarding students' education records.[9] FERPA requires states to provide the following rights to parents:

- to inspect and review their child's education records maintained by the school.[10]
- to a hearing challenging what is in the student's education record.[11]
- to not have education records released to third parties without the written consent of the parent.[12]

FERPA defines "education records" as those materials maintained by the educational agency or institution, containing personally identifiable information directly related to a student. However, the following are not included in this definition (and therefore not subject to FERPA restrictions):

- oral information based on personal observation or knowledge and not based on an education record (e.g., caseworker contacts child's teacher to seek teacher's observations about the child's classroom behavior).

- records solely possessed by the maker, used only as a personal memory aid and not accessible or revealed to any other person except a temporary substitute for the maker of the record. (e.g., classroom teacher keeps a "cheat sheet" at her desk to remind her of issues related to the students, and it is shared with substitute teachers).
- records of the law enforcement unit of an educational agency or institution.

The law requires written consent from the parent before disclosing education records. However, numerous exceptions exist.[13] The exceptions most relevant to child welfare professionals permit disclosure without prior consent to:

- other school officials, including teachers, with legitimate educational interest in the child;[14]
- appropriate persons in connection with an emergency, when the information is needed to protect the health and safety of the student or other persons[15] (Note: this is to be used for health and safety emergencies where immediate release of the information is necessary to control a serious situation);
- officials of other schools when a student is transferring schools;[16]
- state and local authorities within the department of juvenile justice, if your state has a statute permitting this disclosurex[17] (Note: only two states, Florida and Illinois, have such statutes); and
- appropriate persons when the release of information is needed to comply with a judicial order or subpoena.[18]

Additionally, once the information is disclosed, no one can redisclose the information, unless the redisclosure fits under one of the FERPA exceptions.

School systems that repeatedly violate FERPA's disclosure restrictions risk losing federal education funds.[19] While a parent has a right to file a complaint with the U.S. Department of Education for a FERPA violation, parents do not have a private cause of action against a school system for these violations.[20]

Practice Tips:

- Determine if a parent is maintaining contact with the child's school and/or ensuring the child's education needs are being met.
- Seek parental consent to obtain access to education records.
- If the parent is unavailable, or refuses to consent to the release of education information, determine if another individual or agency is considered to be the parent under FERPA (see sidebar #1).
- Look to the exceptions to parental consent permitting disclosure (e.g., compliance with a court order or subpoena).[21]
- For information about how FERPA relates to the delinquency system to obtain access to records, see Sharing Information; *A Guide to the Family Educational Rights and Privacy Act and Participation in Juvenile Justice Programs*, by the U.S. Department of Justice, Office of Justice Programs, Office of Juvenile Justice and Delinquency Prevention, June 1997. Available at http://www.ncjrs.org/pdffiles/163705.pdf.

Accessing Education Records: Defining the "Parent"

Accessing education records in child welfare situations is complicated when the "parent" is unclear.

How FERPA defines "parent"

FERPA statute: uses the term "parent" exclusively when talking about their rights under the law, without defining the term.

FERPA regulations: define parent as "a parent of a student and includes a natural parent, a guardian, or an individual acting as a parent in the absence of a parent or guardian."[1]

Tips for advocates

When facing a FERPA issue, consult state statutes to see if any address accessing student records when children are in care (e.g., some states define "parent" to include the child welfare agency when the agency is the child's custodian[2]).

If your jurisdiction lacks a statute, you will need to interpret whether foster parents and/or the agency fit FERPA's definition of "an individual acting as a parent."

Use an analogy to divorce/custody cases. FERPA regulations clearly state that an educational agency or institution shall give full rights under the act to either parent, unless the agency or institution has been shown a court order, state statute, or legally binding document specifically revoking these rights.[3] Arguably, this provision means that parents, even in child welfare situations, retain their rights under FERPA. Parents retain these rights, even if a child welfare representative also has FERPA rights, unless a court has revoked the parent's rights.

Sources:
[1] 34 C.F.R. § 99.3

[2] Bussiere, et al. *Sharing Information: A Guide to Federal Laws on Confidentiality and Disclosure of Information for Child Welfare Agencies.* Washington, DC: ABA Center on Children and the Law, 1997, 29.

[3] 34 C.F.R. § 99.4

CHILDREN WITH DISABILITIES
Individuals with Disabilities Education Act

The Education for All Handicapped Children's Act was passed in 1975,[22] and renamed the Individuals with Disabilities Education Act (IDEA) in 1990.[23] The IDEA provides that all children with disabilities that impact their ability to make educational progress have a right to a free appropriate public education (FAPE) in the least restrictive environment (LRE) possible. The LRE requirement ensures children with disabilities receive instruction with their non-disabled peers to the maximum extent possible.

Appropriate education

To be "appropriate," an educational program that meets the child's unique education needs must be in place for each child with a disability. In **Board of Education of Hendrick Hudson School District v. Rowley**, 458 U.S. 176 (1982), parents of a deaf child requested a sign language interpreter for their daughter to benefit fully from her regular classroom instruction. The Supreme Court ruled that an "appropriate" education, as required under IDEA, does not require that the student reach her maximum potential, but only required that she have a reasonable opportunity to learn. The court determined that because the student could derive *some educational benefit* in her regular classroom without the interpreter, there was no requirement that the school provide the additional service. As a result of **Rowley**, courts have generally interpreted "some educational benefit" to mean "meaningful educational progress."

Individualized education program

A child qualifies for IDEA services if school personnel and the child's parents identifies the child as having one or more disabilities, such as a learning disability, emotional disturbance, physical disability, or autism that impacts on the child's ability to make educational progress. An education plan then must be developed for the child. The education plan must result in a written individualized education program (IEP) tailored to each child's needs. The IEP identifies goals and objectives, necessary accommodations or modifications, and related services. (Chapter 3 discusses your role in the special education process and how it affects you and your client.)

Related services

The U.S. Supreme Court has clarified what constitutes a "related service" under the IDEA. In **Cedar Rapids Community School District v. Garret F.**, 526 U.S. 66 (1999), the Court determined that nursing care for a child needing a ventilator was a related service under IDEA. The Court held that if a medical doctor is not required to provide the service, and the service is necessary for the child to benefit from special education, then the school system must provide the service.[24]

Transition services

By the time the child is 14, the IEP team determines what transition services are needed to prepare the child for adulthood and the future. These services can include: post-secondary education, vocational training, integrated services, independent living, or community participation. These services are based on the individual student's needs, taking into account the student's preferences and interests.[25]

Surrogate parents

When a child is in foster care, it is necessary to determine who is acting as the parent, and therefore whose rights are protected under IDEA. IDEA provides for the appointment of a surrogate parent to make educational decisions for certain situations, including when a child is in foster care. Federal law states if a child is a "ward of the state" and has a disability, or is being considered for special education services, states must put procedures in place to protect the rights of these children, including assessing the need for and appointing a surrogate.[26] (Chapter 3 discusses parent surrogates in more depth.)

Practice Tips:

- Identify those children in foster care with disabilities, both diagnosed and undiagnosed.
- Talk with the child, when developmentally appropriate, to discuss the child's feelings about the disability and special education services.
- Understand the benefits afforded under IDEA, and, when appropriate, advocate for children in foster care to receive all the services through the school system to which they are legally entitled.
- Determine who is the education decision maker.
- Determine if a surrogate parent is needed, and if so ensure that an appropriate and knowledgeable individual is appointed.

Section 504 of the Rehabilitation Act

Passed in 1973, Section 504 prohibits discrimination against individuals with disabilities in all programs receiving federal funding.[27] While Section 504 is an antidis-

crimination law, not an education law, its regulations apply to preschool, elementary, and secondary programs that receive any kind of federal funds that support their programs.[28] These regulations prohibit specific discriminatory practices, and require schools to be proactive in ensuring students with disabilities receive an appropriate education. Unlike many laws discussed in this chapter, no federal funding accompanies this law.

Under Section 504, an "individual with a disability" is someone who:

- has a physical or mental impairment which substantially limits one or more major life activities;[29]
- has a record of such impairment; or
- is regarded as having such an impairment.[30]

Section 504 requires schools to meet with parents to discuss and evaluate a child's disability, determine eligibility, and make a decision about services and accommodations. Extended time on tests, use of a computer for assignments, and tutoring are types of accommodations available to students under Section 504. Parents who are dissatisfied with the determinations may file a complaint with the U.S. Department of Education's Office of Civil Rights, take the case to an administrative hearing, or file a civil action.

All students who are eligible for services under IDEA are also eligible for services under Section 504. Accommodations and services provided under Section 504 are typically incorporated into the IEP of an IDEA-eligible student. However, some children who are not eligible under IDEA, may still be eligible for Section 504 services. This is because to qualify under IDEA a student must need specially tailored instruction to address the disability that is impeding academic progress, while under Section 504 the disability must affect a major life activity.[31] Therefore, Section 504 applies to a larger pool of children with disabilities than IDEA. (See sidebar #2.)

Practice Tips:

- Understand decision-making is determined under Section 504 when a child is in foster care, as the federal statute and regulations do not address the definition of parent or issues involving foster care.
- Understand and advocate for services and protections under Section 504 for children with disabilities.
- Remember to consider Section 504 eligibility for those children found not eligible for IDEA services and protections.

FAIR SCHOOL DISCIPLINE

Although all children have the right to attend school, this does not override the school's authority to discipline a child for misconduct, including suspensions and expulsions.

Short-Term Suspensions

In **Goss v. Lopez,**[32] the U.S. Supreme Court held that minimum protections of procedural due process must be provided to students suspended for 10 days or less. These protections are:

- oral or written notice of the specific violation the student is charged with and the intended punishment.
- an opportunity to refute the charges against the student before an impartial decision maker.
- an explanation of the evidence the disciplinarian relied upon.[33]

Long-Term Suspensions and Expulsions

While *Goss* clarified the minimum requirements for short-term suspensions, the Court provided little guidance regarding due process rights for longer, and more critical, disciplinary actions of long-term suspensions and expulsions. Absent federal authority to help states determine procedures for these significant disciplinary measures, most states have required schools to have more formal due process procedures for long-term suspensions and expulsions than the requirements for short-term suspensions in *Goss.*[34] Many school districts have developed their own policies regarding these disciplinary measures.

The **Federal Gun-Free Schools Act** was passed in 1994, beginning the wave of "zero tolerance" laws and policies relating to violence in schools.[35] This act mandates a one-year expulsion for students who bring a firearm to school, and requires schools to refer the offending student to the criminal or juvenile justice system. However, the law allows the "child administrative officer," usually the school superintendent, to modify the mandatory expulsion on a case-by-case basis, allowing for administrative discretion when imposing this sanction.[36]

Discipline for Students with Disabilities

Section 504 and IDEA require special disciplinary procedures for students with disabilities.[37] Children qualifying under these laws may still receive disciplinary sanctions, up to 10 days of suspension for a school year, similar to their nondisabled peers. However, once a disabled student has missed 10 days of school because of disciplinary measures, different rules may

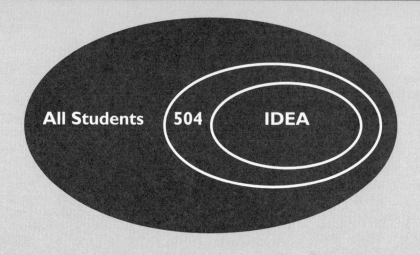

All Students 504 **IDEA**

The Interplay Between IDEA and Section 504:
Not all students have disabilities. Of those students who have disabilities, most will qualify for Section 504 services, but only some of those students with disabilities will qualify for IDEA services.

apply.[38] Chapter 5 details these rules, the discipline process, and programs that are available to ensure discipline does not interfere with the educations of these youth.

Practice Tips:

- Familiarize yourself with state laws and school district disciplinary policies.
- When appropriate, ensure the disciplinary decision maker accounts for the fact that the child is in the foster care system, or the circumstances leading to foster placement when deciding what discipline to impose.
- Federal law, as well as some state and local disciplinary policies, allows school administrators to retain some discretionary power in determining sanctions for disciplinary violations. When an administrator has authority to review situations on a case-by-case basis, advocates should bring all of a child's unique circumstances, such as history of abuse or neglect, to their attention, when appropriate.

- The child's privacy rights must be considered and you may need to (and depending on your role, may be required to) consult with the child before revealing personal details to school personnel.

- Ensure that a disabled child in foster care who violates the disciplinary code, but has not been found disabled, does not receive unnecessary and/or inappropriate punishments. There is a much higher risk of long-term suspension or expulsion because the child's disabilities have never been identified and the school will not follow the special manifestation hearing procedures. (Chapter 5 discusses this situation, and suggests how advocates can handle these cases.)

- Remember that whether a child in foster care has a disability or not, disciplinary actions can be devastating for the child's future. Many youth in care, on the fence about continuing in school, leave school permanently following a suspension or expulsion.

QUALITY EDUCATION AND SAFE SCHOOLS
No Child Left Behind Act of 2001 (NCLB)

The NCLB, signed into law in January 2002, reauthorized the Elementary and Secondary Education Act.[39] The new law focuses on such issues as annual testing, better teacher qualifications, and changes for low-performing schools. Of interest to child welfare advocates are two provisions for students attending schools that fail to meet state standards, and a third provision for students attending "persistently dangerous" schools.

First, children attending schools that have been designated "in need of improvement" for two consecutive years (including the years before the new law was enacted) must be given the opportunity to attend better public (including charter) schools. The schools are required to pay for transportation to the new schools.

Second, schools that fail to meet state standards for at least three of the four previous years, must make "supplemental educational services" (e.g., tutoring and academic support) available to low-income students. These services must be paid for by the school and be provided outside of regular school hours. Parents and students may select their own providers, but these providers must meet certain state standards.

Another noteworthy NCLB provision emphasizes keeping schools safe and drug free. States must allow students who attend persistently dangerous schools, or who have been victimized by school violence, to transfer to a safe school. States determine their own definition of "persistently dangerous." Safety statistics must be reported to the public for each school in the district, and schools must implement drug and violence prevention programs.

Advocates may need to take steps to ensure that these school transfer options and supplemental services are available to eligible children in the foster care system.

Practice Tips:

- Obtain information about the schools in your districts to determine which have been designated as "in need of improvement" and determine how many years they have held this status.
- Obtain safety statistics for the schools in your district and determine which school has been identified as "persistently dangerous."
- Consult http://nclb.ecs.org/nclb/ to find information about your state NCLB provisions.
- Explore which outside tutoring programs in your community meet the state standards.
- Advocate for school transfers and/or additional services for those students who are entitled.

SCHOOL STABILITY AND ENROLLMENT

McKinney-Vento Homeless Assistance Act

Passed in 1987, and most recently amended as part of the No Child Left Behind Act of 2001, this law provides federal money to states to "ensure that children and youth in homeless situations receive a free, appropriate public education."[40] The law aims to remove obstacles that delay enrollment or prevent access to public education for homeless students, such as: residency requirements; mandatory documentation requirements prior to enrollment, such as education, medical and immunization records, or birth certificates; proof of guardianship requirements; and lack of transportation to school.[41] Children covered under this law must be immediately enrolled in school, even if these typical requirements for school enrollment are not fulfilled. The law permits students to continue their education at their home school, even if they have been moved from the home school jurisdiction. Students may also re-enroll at a new, more convenient school.

The new 2001 amendments to this law make the following youth eligible under the act: "...children and youth who are...living in emergency or transitional shelters; are abandoned in hospitals; or are awaiting foster care placement..."[42] There is no federal definition of "awaiting foster care placement." States are free to determine a definition of this term in a way that makes certain youth in foster care who are not in stable placements eligible under the law. In this way, the McKinney-Vento Act can be an important tool when advocating for immediate admission into school for children in foster care.

Practice Tips:

- Notify the McKinney-Vento liaison for the school district when working with a child that fits this definition and needs immediate school access.
- Talk with the student about the options (e.g., remaining in home school, or moving to a new, closer school) and determine which school to access.
- For more information about enrolling a child in school under McKinney-Vento, visit the National Law Center on Homelessness and Poverty web site, for a step-by-step guide: http://www.nlchp.org/FA_Education/BackToSchoolAdvocacy.html.

FEDERAL PRESCHOOL PROGRAMS

Children between birth and five years need education services just as much as older children. These early years are critical in a young child's development, and early education is an important precursor for future school success. Several federal programs may be accessed for young children in foster care.

Early and Periodic Screening, Diagnosis and Treatment (EPSDT)

This program mandates comprehensive health services for all Medicaid-eligible children from birth through 18 years. The law requires four periodic screens: medical, vision, hearing, and dental. The medical screen must include a complete health and developmental history, including assessments of physical and mental health development. The health care required under EPSDT includes complete age and developmentally appropriate physical exams. EPSDT also covers "necessary diagnostic and treatment services to correct or ameliorate defects and physical and mental illness and conditions discovered by the screen."[43]

Head Start/Early Head Start

This program began in 1965, but has evolved and expanded over the years. Last amended by the Head Start Act in 1998, this program provides full education services to low-income families, including health, nutrition, and social services for children and their families.[45] Children must be at least three years old to be eligible for Head Start.[46] Head Start programs must screen children to identify developmental, mental, sensory, behavioral, motor, language, social, cognitive, perceptual, and emotional skills issues.[47] If issues exist, appropriate medical services and follow-up treatment must be arranged.[48] Furthermore, the programs must be implemented in a developmentally appropriate way, taking into account the backgrounds and learning abilities of the children.[49]

In 1995, Head Start expanded to include Early Head Start, a program for pregnant women and families with infants and toddlers up to age three. The program provides intensive services, beginning before the child is born, and focuses on enhancing the child's development and supporting the family during the child's critical first three years.

IDEA Early Intervention Services

In 1986, the Education of All Handicapped Children's Act (precursor to the IDEA) was amended to require states to provide programs and services to children who are disabled (or are suspected of having a disability). These services begin at birth, rather than age three, as the original law provided.[51] The law, found under **Part C of IDEA**, requires states to serve children between zero and three years who are: (1) diagnosed with a mental or physical disability that has a high probability of resulting in developmental delay, and (2) developmentally delayed according to state criteria.[52] States may include young children at risk of developmental delay in the group of children that qualify for services under Part C.

Under IDEA Part C, services are provided to the child and family of the young child through an individualized family service plan (IFSP), which is created with input from the child's family. Children can receive services such as physical, occupational, or speech therapy, transportation, special instruction, or be provided such aides as assistive technology devices, wheelchairs, or hearing aids.[53] The law further requires some kind of service coordination, such as a case manager.[54] IDEA Part C also provides for the appointment of parent surrogates for children in foster care (See earlier discussion of parent surrogates).

- Determine if infant and toddler services under IDEA are appropriate to aid young children in foster care with disabilities, developmental delays, or who have a high probability of developmental delays.
- Work with the school system to obtain these services for eligible foster children.
- If your state includes the "at risk" category for children eligible for services under IDEA Part C, consider whether young children who have been the victims of child abuse and neglect may benefit from early intervention services and ensure that the referral process is initiated.
- Determine the education decision maker, be it the parent or other individual. Under Part C, parents can reject services and there is no procedure available for the school to require the parent to accept the help. Therefore, determining the education decision maker in these situations is critical.
- Determine if a surrogate parent is needed, and if so ensure that an appropriate and knowledgeable individual is appointed.

TEENAGERS

No federal law addresses how long a child must remain in school. State laws differ on this requirement, as well as on the age that a child has a RIGHT to an education versus the age at which a child MUST be in school.[55] For example, in Maryland, children have the right to an education until age 21, but that child only is required to attend school until age 16.[56] Since laws in many states do not require children to attend school beyond 15 or 16 years of age, it is imperative that the child welfare system has a means to encourage teens in care to remain in school.

Foster Care Independence Act of 1999 (FCIA)[57]

This act helps children who are likely to leave the child welfare system at age 18 continue their education, find employment, and obtain life skills to be successful adults. It doubles the amount of federal funds (Chafee funds) provided to the states for services to older teens, and gives states increased flexibility in using the funds. For example, states can use Chafee funds to aid education goals in the following ways: tuition, tutoring, education planning, financial aid, and other education expenses related to receiving a high school diploma, GED, or post-secondary education.

Tuition Waivers

Many states offer tuition waivers for current and/or former foster youth, and have done so since before the FCIA was passed. For a list of which states offer these waivers, and the details of the state waiver, visit the National Resource Center on Youth Development's web site at http://www.ncrys.ou.edu/TuitionWaivers/ USMap.htm.

Education and Training Vouchers (ETVs)

An amendment to the Promoting Safe and Stable Families Act, passed in early 2002, authorized additional funds for education and training voucher programs for youth aging out of foster care and youth adopted from foster care after reaching age 16.[58] This program will provide these youth with vouchers up to $5,000 per year for education and training, including post-secondary training. The voucher amount would not be considered when determining a youth's eligibility for other federal education assistance benefits.

Transfer of Rights at 18

FERPA gives teenagers over age 18 additional control of their educations. Under FERPA, if a student is 18 years or older, rights transfer to, and consent to the release of records must come from, the student. However notices of disclosure are sent to the parent and child. Under IDEA, states can transfer rights to children 18 years and older, unless the student is determined to be incompetent or unable to provide informed consent.[59]

Practice Tips:

- Know the laws in your state regarding the age children are required to be in school and the age children have the right to be in school.
- Know how Chafee funds can be used, and advocate using these funds to help older youth in your community.
- Be creative. One jurisdiction in Florida uses Chafee funds to provide com-

puter-training classes to foster youth. Youth who complete the class receive a laptop computer, also paid for with Chafee funds.

- Advocate for youth to access ETVs for higher education pursuits.
- Learn if your state offers tuition waivers for current and/or former foster children. Be alert for news about the funding for new education and training voucher programs.
- Remember that some state waiver programs, and the education and training voucher program, apply to current foster youth as well as older youth who are already adopted.
- Inform youth over age 18 of their additional education rights.

CONCLUSION

A solid grasp of the core federal laws governing education will prepare you to spot issues and identify needs for advocacy. As always, consult your state law for additional clarification. Remaining chapters address several of the areas touched on in this chapter: special education process, disciplinary procedures, and services for young children.

Endnotes

[1] All 50 states have such laws. These rights are typically found in state constitutions, but can also be found in state statutes.

[2] This includes public or private school, and in some states home schooling, as long as certain requirements are met.

[3] Kramer, Donald. *The Legal Rights of Children (2)*, Second Edition. Colorado Springs: Shepard's /McGraw –Hill, Inc, 1994, 438.

[4] The right to attend school is subject to the exception of disciplinary consequences that result in the child's removal from school (see disciplinary discussion later in the chapter).

[5] The provisions that most affect the rights of children in public schools include: the First Amendment (freedom of speech, religion, and association); the Fourth Amendment (freedom from unreasonable searches and seizures); and the Fourteenth Amendment (the right to due process of law and equal protection of the laws). Kramer, 1994, 435.

[6] Plyler v. Doe, 457 U.S. 202 (1982).

[7] Some states have bona fide religious belief exceptions. Also see provisions of the McKinney-Vento Act, dealing with homeless children, discussed later in the article.

[8] Kramer, 1994, 611. To do so would violate the girls' constitutional rights as well as violate Title IX (20 U.S.C. §§ 1681-1686; 34 C.F.R. § 106.40(b)).

[9] 20 U.S.C. § 1232g; 34 C.F.R. § 99. FERPA has been amended several times since its enactment in 1974, most recently by the No Child Left Behind Act of 2000.

[10] 20 U.S.C. § 1232g (a)(1)(A). The law requires states to establish procedures for giving parents access to this information, which can be no later than 45 days after a request is made. In addition to FERPA, IDEA also specifies a parent's right to a child's education records. 20 U.S.C. § 1415(b)(1).

[11] 20 U.S.C. § 1232g (a)(2). This hearing can result in correction, deletion, or insertion of information if the record is inaccurate, misleading, or violates the student's privacy rights.

[12] 20 U.S.C. § 1232g(b).

[13] For a complete list of exceptions, refer to the FERPA statute and regulations.

[14] 20 U.S.C. § 1232g(b)(1)(A).

[15] 20 U.S.C. § 1232g(b)(1)(I).

[16] 20 U.S.C. § 1232g(b)(1)(B).

[17] 20 U.S.C. § 1232g(b)(1)(E). To date, only Illinois and Florida have adopted such statutes.

[18] 20 U.S.C. § 1232g(b)(1)(J).

[19] 20 U.S.C. § 1232g(f). To date, no state has ever lost federal funding for violating FERPA.

[20] Gonzaga v. John Doe, 536 U.S. 273 (2002) (Supreme Court ruled that students and parents may not sue for damages under 42 U.S.C. § 1983 to enforce provisions of the Family Educational Rights and Privacy Act (FERPA)).

[21] 20 U.S.C. § 1232g(b)(1)(J).

[22] Pub. L. No. 94-142.

[23] IDEA was most recently amended in 1997, and should be reauthorized in 2004.

[24] In an earlier case, the U.S. Supreme Court decided Irving Independent School District v. Tatro, 468 U.S. 883 (1984). This case involved a student with spina bifida who required intermittent catheterization throughout the day to remain at school. The Court held that this was a related service under the IDEA and that the school nurse needed to perform the procedure.

[25] 20 U.S.C. § 1401(30).

[26] Individuals with Disabilities Education Act, 20 U.S.C. § 1415(b)(2); 34 C.F.R. § 300.515.

[27] 29 U.S.C. § 794.

[28] 34 C.F.R. § 104.

[29] Learning is considered a major life activity.

[30] 34 C.F.R. § 104.3(j).

[31] "Major life activities" means functions such as caring for oneself, performing manual tasks, walking, seeing, hearing, speaking, breathing, learning and working. 34 C.F.R. § 104(3)(j)(2)(ii).

[32] 49 U.S. 565 (1975).

[33] Brady, Kevin. "Weapon of Choice: Zero Tolerance School Discipline Policies and the Limitations of Student Procedural Due Process." Children's Legal Rights Journal 22(1), Spring 2002, 4.

[34] Ibid.

[35] 20 U.S.C. § 7151.

[36] Brady, 2002, 9 n.19.

[37] Case law preceded the codification of these special disciplinary procedures, most notably Honig v. Doe, 484 U.S. 305 (1988) (established that a student qualifying for special education services could not be expelled from school indefinitely if the student's behavior related to the student's disability).

[38] 20 U.S.C. § 1415(k); 34 C.F.R. § 300.519-300.529.

[39] No Child Left Behind Act of 2001, 20 U.S.C. § 6301.

[40] Ibid., § 1031 et seq.

[41] For an in-depth discussion of the McKinney-Vento Act, see Julianelle, Patricia. "The New McKinney-Vento Act: Promoting Student Achievement Through Educational Stability." *Children's Legal Rights Journal* 22(1), Spring 2002.

[42] 42 U.S.C. § 11434a(2).

[43] 42 U.S.C. § 1396d(r)(5).

[44] See Pediatric Specialty Care, Inc. v. Arkansas Dep't of Human Servs, 293 F.3d 472 (8th Cir. 2002) (children eligible for Medicaid have a federal right to early intervention day treatment services); Westside Mothers v. Haveman, 289 F.3d 852 (6th Cir. 2002) (state officials can be sued in federal court for failing to provide EPSDT services).

[45] 42 U.S.C. § 9831 et seq.

[46] 45 C.F.R. § 1305.4(a).

[47] 45 C.F.R. §1304.20(b).

[48] 45 C.F.R. §1304.20(a)(iii-iv); 45 C.F.R. §1304.20(c).

[49] 45 C.F.R. §1304.21(a).

[50] Federal law does not require Head Start programs to make children in the child welfare system a priority.

[51] Pub. L. No. 99-457.

[52] 20 U.S.C. § 1431 et seq.

[53] For more on IDEA Part C eligibility and services, see Dicker, Sheryl & Elysa Gordon. "Opening the Door to Early Intervention for Abused and Neglected Children: A New CAPTA Requirement." *ABA Child Law Practice* 23(3), May 2004, 33; Dicker, Sheryl. "Early Intervention and Early Childhood Programs: Essential Tools for Child Welfare Advocacy." *Clearinghouse Review Journal of Poverty Law and Policy* 34(11-12), March-April 2001, 727.

[54] In fact, the money provided under IDEA Part C is specifically intended for this case coordination component. The actual services are typically paid through Medicaid.

[55] Kramer, 1994, 447.

[56] Md. Educ. § 7-101, 7-301.

[57] Pub. L. No. 106-169, codified under Title IV-E of the Social Security Act.

[58] Program was funded for $42 million in the 2003 budget and signed into law on February 20, 2003.

[59] For more on this issue, see Rebore, Deborah. "Transfer of Rights Under the Individuals with Disabilities Act: Adulthood With Ability or Disability?" *Bringham Young University Education and Law Journal*, 2000, 33.

NAVIGATING THE SPECIAL EDUCATION PROCESS

INTRODUCTION

Of the more than 500,000 children in foster care, approximately 30-40% are receiving special education services.[1] Many others may need these services, but have not been identified. Still others have been identified inappropriately. As an advocate in the child welfare system, you need to know how the special education system works and understand the benefits and services that can be accessed for children in foster care. By understanding the federal Individuals with Disabilities Education Act (IDEA),[2] which governs the special education process, you can help the child welfare system provide education services for children with disabilities.

This chapter answers common questions about how the special education process works and the issues that arise for children in the foster care system. It also provides tips on navigating the special education system and ensuring the process benefits children in foster care. The questions and answers are listed in order of how issues may arise in each step of the special education process.

What Signs Should I Look for That a Child Needs Special Education Services?

While some children in foster care may have apparent disabilities (e.g., orthopedic impairments), other disabilities are not easy to identify. For less obvious disabilities, such as learning impairments, look for subtle signs of problems. In addition to obtaining information about family medical history, watch for signs that the child is having school difficulties, such as:

- poor grades
- delays in academic achievements or developmental milestones
- lack of interest in school
- refusal to attend school
- behavior problems at school and at home

If you observe these signs, get professional opinions about their causes. While not all children who show one or more of these signs will qualify for special education services, without your follow through a child with possible needs may never be identified. Children in the child welfare system often already have counselors or therapists who may supply information that will help identify causes of concerning behaviors.

What Do I Do if I Suspect a Child Needs Special Education Services, But is Not Yet Identified?

You have two options:

1. Conduct an independent investigation. Before getting the school involved, especially if you have concerns that the school may move too slowly (or too quickly) to identify the child as needing special education services without a legitimate basis, consider an intermediate step. Over- and underidentifying children in foster care as needing special education services are problems. Therefore, before involving the school, find out if someone outside the school system has already conducted a thorough evaluation.

If no, or not enough evaluation data exists, seek a thorough evaluation, or additional evaluations, of the child by a clinician familiar with educational disabilities. You will have to determine what types of evaluations are needed, which may require outside expertise. For example, in addition to educational testing, you may want a physical health evaluation or a neurological evaluation by a medical doctor, or a psychological or psychosocial evaluation by a clinical psychologist, or some combination of these and other evaluations. (See Appendix D for more on education testing.) The child welfare agency would need to pay for these evaluations,[3] either voluntarily or perhaps through an order from the child welfare judge instructing the child welfare agency to arrange and pay for them.

Consider arranging an in-school observation of the child in the classroom; the school system should allow a qualified individual to conduct such an observation. Review the evaluation reports, and all information from other professionals involved with the child, to determine whether enough documentation establishes the need to move forward with a request for special education services. Be sure to review the legal definitions for the various disabilities under the federal IDEA (34 C.F.R. § 300.7) (see sidebar #2) and

Case #1: Alan

(Child May Need Special Education Services but is Not Yet Evaluated)

- Alan has been in a regular third grade classroom for three weeks in a new school after being removed from his mom and placed in a foster home.

- Alan's caseworker comes to Alan's classroom and observes him sitting in the back of the room with his head down on his desk during the teacher's lesson. The caseworker asks to see some classwork and is shown several examples for which Alan received failing grades.

- The foster mother reports to the caseworker that she is struggling to get Alan to complete his homework. Alan will rarely sit still long enough to get through an assignment.

- The foster mom has to let Alan take breaks every 15 minutes to get through his evening homework. The assignments are taking so long to complete that Alan is staying up later at night than the foster mom would like, trying to complete the work.

What Should the Caseworker Do?

Alan needs to be evaluated, either privately or through the school system (see "What Do I Do If I Suspect a Child Needs Special Education Services But is Not Yet Identified?" in this chapter for discussion of these two options). Alan could:

- have attention issues or an undiagnosed learning disability,

- be depressed about his recent removal from his parents,

- be tired in class because of his late nights trying to complete homework,

- be lost in class because his previous school curriculum does not have him up to speed with where his new class is academically.

He could have all or just one or two of these issues. Some of them could mean he needs special education services, but some may not. The only way to determine the right way to help Alan is a good, thorough evaluation. Once a quality evaluation is conducted, the evaluation should be reviewed by the school team to determine if special education services are warranted.

Sidebar 1 Special Education and Section 504: A Roadmap

This chart highlights the main steps to the special education and Section 504 processes. Always consult federal and state laws, regulations, and policies.

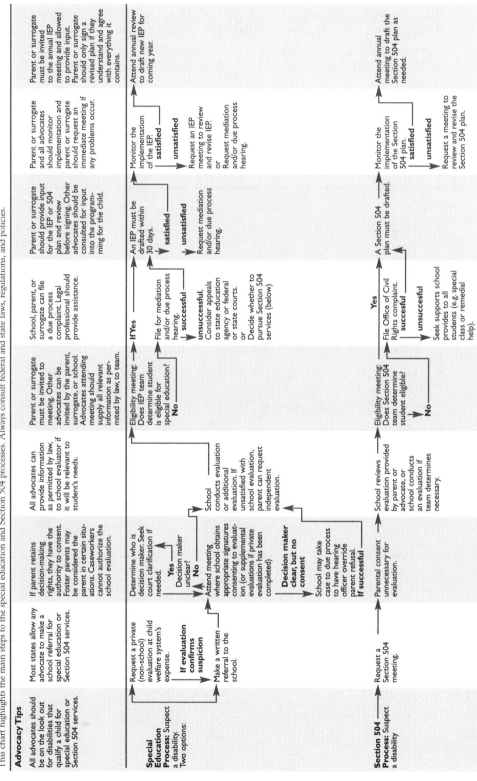

state law, and consult other professionals who know about special education practice to determine if the documented evidence might support your request for special education services.

This type of strategy has three benefits:

- it allows you to have a good idea of your desired outcome when you contact the school system to seek services. In other words, when you get aboard the special education train, you already know where you want it to stop.
- if appropriate outside evaluations can be accessed more quickly by the child welfare agency, this may speed the identification process.
- it arms you with good evaluative materials to combat the school system, should it not agree with your assessment. This could save time later.

A disadvantage to this strategy is that it may delay getting the ball rolling with the school system, as the school will still have the right to review your evaluations and conduct its own independent evaluations. The school will still be entitled to the same time period to conduct these additional evaluations as they would have to conduct all of the evaluations. While one goal of this strategy is to save time, there is no guarantee that it will. Also, the child welfare system in this scenario is responsible for the cost of the original evaluation.

If you choose this option, inform the school in writing that you have conducted outside evaluations of the child that you want the school to review, and that you believe the child needs special education services. If you plan to do an in-school observation, call the school in advance to

arrange a suitable time to observe the student. Remember, in this situation the school has the right to review your evaluation and conduct its own independent evaluations. Ultimately, eligibility under IDEA will be a team decision and cannot be predetermined.

2. Make a formal, written request to the school for a full evaluation of the child. This second option puts the responsibility for obtaining evaluations of the child solely on the school system. This is appropriate for situations when there are no resources to pursue outside evaluations, or when parties involved are comfortable using the evaluation services offered by the school. Put another way, these are situations where you are comfortable getting on the special education train without knowing where it is going to stop.

With this option, your first action needs to be a written request to the school to evaluate the child. Consult your state law to determine who is permitted to make such a request; most states permit any advocate to do so. This request should be in writing to clearly document your actions. Consider using certified mail to have an official receipt of your correspondence. Keep copies of every document you send the school for your records. This documentation may be needed later if you need to challenge the school system for failing to complete the evaluation process promptly.

As a result of the request, the school should convene a meeting and seek written consent of the parent to proceed with the evaluation.

Definitions of Disabilities under IDEA

These are the federal definitions of disabilities under IDEA. Be sure to check your state laws and regulations for variations in these definitions and other terms used.

34 C.F.R. §300.7 Child with a disability.

(c) Definitions of disability terms. The terms used in this definition are defined as follows:

(1)(i) **Autism** means a developmental disability significantly affecting verbal and nonverbal communication and social interaction, generally evident before age 3, that adversely affects a child's educational performance. Other characteristics often associated with autism are engagement in repetitive activities and stereo-typed movements, resistance to environmental change or change in daily routines, and unusual responses to sensory experiences. The term does not apply if a child's educational performance is adversely affected primarily because the child has an emotional disturbance,

(ii) A child who manifests the characteristics of "autism" after age 3 could be diagnosed as having "autism" if the criteria in paragraph (c)(1)(i) of this section are satisfied.

(2) **Deaf blindness** means concomitant hearing and visual impairments, the combination of which causes such severe communication and other developmental and educational needs that they cannot be accommodated in special education programs solely for children with deafness or children with blindness.

(3) **Deafness** means a hearing impairment that is so severe that the child is impaired in processing linguistic information through hearing, with or without amplification, that adversely affects a child's educational performance.

(4) **Emotional disturbance** is defined as follows:

(i) The term means a condition exhibiting one or more of the following characteristics over a long period of time and to a marked degree that adversely affects a child's educational performance:

(A) An inability to learn that cannot be explained by intellectual, sensory, or health factors.

(B) An inability to build or maintain satisfactory interpersonal relationships with peers and teachers.

(C) Inappropriate types of behavior or feelings under normal circumstances.

(D) A general pervasive mood of unhappiness or depression.

(E) A tendency to develop physical symptoms or fears associated with personal or school problems.

(ii) The term includes schizophrenia. The term does not apply to children who are socially maladjusted, unless it is determined that they have an emotional disturbance.

(5) **Hearing impairment** means an impairment in hearing, whether permanent or fluctuating, that adversely affects a child's educational performance but that is not included under the definition of deafness in this section.

(6) **Mental retardation** means significantly subaverage general intellectual functioning, existing concurrently with deficits in adaptive behavior and manifested during the developmental period, that adversely affects a child's educational performance.

(7) **Multiple disabilities** means concomitant impairments (such as mental retardation blindness, mental retardation orthopedic impairment, etc.), the combination of which causes such severe educational needs that they cannot be accommodated in special education programs solely for one of the impairments. The term does not include deafblindness.

(8) **Orthopedic impairment** means a severe orthopedic impairment that adversely affects a child's educational performance. The term includes impairments caused by congenital anomaly (e.g., clubfoot, absence of some member, etc.), impairments caused by disease (e.g., poliomyelitis, bone tuberculosis, etc.), and impairments from other causes (e.g., cerebral palsy, amputations, and fractures or burns that cause contractures).

(9) **Other health impairment** means having limited strength, vitality or alertness, including a heightened alertness to environmental stimuli, that results in limited alertness with respect to the educational environment, that—

(i) Is due to chronic or acute health problems such as asthma, attention deficit disorder or attention deficit hyperactivity disorder, diabetes, epilepsy, a heart condition, hemophilia, lead poisoning, leukemia, nephritis, rheumatic fever, and sickle cell anemia; and

(ii) Adversely affects a child's educational performance.

(10) **Specific learning disability** is defined as follows:

(i) **General.** The term means a disorder in one or more of the basic psychological processes involved in understanding or in using language, spoken or written, that may manifest itself in an imperfect ability to listen, think, speak, read, write, spell, or to do mathematical calculations, including conditions such as perceptual disabilities, brain injury, minimal brain dysfunction, dyslexia, and developmental aphasia.

(ii) **Disorders not included.** The term does not include learning problems that are primarily the result of visual, hearing, or motor disabilities, of mental retardation, of emotional disturbance, or of environmental, cultural, or economic disadvantage.

(11) **Speech or language impairment** means a communication disorder, such as stuttering, impaired articulation, a language impairment, or a voice impairment, that adversely affects a child's educational performance.

(12) **Traumatic brain injury** means an acquired injury to the brain caused by an external physical force, resulting in total or partial functional disability or psychosocial impairment, or both, that adversely affects a child's educational performance. The term applies to open or closed head injuries resulting in impairments in one or more areas, such as cognition; language; memory; attention; reasoning; abstract thinking; judgment; problem solving; sensory, perceptual, and motor abilities; psychosocial behavior; physical functions; information processing; and speech. The term does not apply to brain injuries that are congenital or degenerative, or to brain injuries induced by birth trauma.

(13) **Visual impairment including blindness** means an impairment in vision that, even with correction, adversely affects a child's educational performance. The term includes both partial sight and blindness.

20 U.S.C. § 1401(3)(A) and (B); § 1401(26).

EDUCATION DECISION MAKERS

How Do I Determine Who Can Act as the Parent or if a Surrogate Parent is Needed?

While usually an advocate can request a referral for evaluation of special education needs, only the parent or surrogate can consent to the evaluation or reevaluation of the child, and ultimately to the services put in place for the child. Therefore, when consents for evaluations need to be signed, it must be determined if a parent is available or if a surrogate needs to be appointed. The parent or the surrogate is the key decision maker for all IDEA-related issues, including services and placement, so clarity at the beginning of the process is critical.

The IDEA statute requires states to establish procedural safeguards to ensure children with disabilities receive a free and appropriate public education (FAPE). The law specifically requires procedures to be in place when:

- "the parents of the child are not known,
- the agency cannot, after reasonable efforts locate the parents, or
- the child is a ward of the State."[4]

These procedures need to include the assignment of an individual as the surrogate when needed.[5]

To determine the need for a surrogate you must review the IDEA regulation; it defines parent as a:

- **prong 1** "natural or adoptive parent of the child;
- **prong 2** a guardian, but not the state if the child is a ward of the state;
- **prong 3** a person acting in the place of a parent (such as a grandparent or step-parent with whom the child lives, or a person who is legally responsible for the child's welfare; or
- **prong 4** a surrogate parent..."[6]

Based on the four prongs of this definition, you can argue under the second and third prong that guardians and relative caretakers or anyone with legal custody of a child (other than the state) have the same rights as a parent under IDEA. In some states foster parents are considered the parents under this third prong and do not need to be appointed as surrogates (see next section). It may be wise to get a court order to memorialize this legal arrangement.

Children in foster care without a person fitting the first three prongs of the definition of parent above, will need a surrogate parent. A surrogate parent sits in the shoes of the parents and makes decisions about special education services for the child. Federal law leaves the specific process of appointing a surrogate up to states. Consult state law, regulations, and policies to find out how your state appoints a surrogate when one is needed for a child in foster care.

Who Can be Appointed As A Surrogate for a Child in Foster Care?

Some states require anyone acting as the parent (people that fit under the third prong) to be officially appointed as a surrogate parent (under the forth prong), to make their role as the education decision maker even clearer. Be sure to consult your state law to determine the best way for these individuals to have the authority to be the child's decision maker.

Federal law is clear that a surrogate parent cannot be an employee of the state education agency, the lead education agency, or any other agency that is involved in the education or care of the child.[7] Therefore, child welfare agency personnel, including caseworkers, cannot be the surrogate parent for a child in foster care.

It is preferable that a surrogate be a person who knows about the child's needs. If the education decision maker cannot be the parent, guardian, or person acting in place of the parent, the next best option is to have a surrogate appointed who has some knowledge of the child. This may be the foster parent, a relative, a court appointed special advocate (CASA),[8] a child's attorney or guardian ad litem, or some other person involved in the child's life. The appropriateness of the individual will differ from state to state, and even from case to case. Preferably, the individual will understand the special education process, or at least be willing to learn and work with someone who can guide them through the process. For example, a relative may agree to be the surrogate, with assurances that the child's attorney will attend meetings and help advocate for the

Case #2: Betty
(Foster Parent as Education Surrogate)

- Betty was placed in the foster home of Mrs. Smith two weeks ago.

- Betty's permanency plan has been changed to adoption, but parental rights have not yet been terminated.

- Mrs. Smith is the mother of an adult son who has a severe learning disability and she has spent years advocating for him in the school system.

- Mrs. Smith is willing to adopt Betty once parental rights are terminated.

- Betty is in special education and her previous foster mom had been her surrogate parent, but now that Betty has left her home, she no longer wants to serve in that role.

Can Mrs. Smith be Betty's Surrogate?

The answer will depend on state law. In some jurisdictions, the answer will likely be yes. The fact that the previous foster parent had been appointed as surrogate leads us to believe that this jurisdiction allows foster parents to be appointed as surrogates, and that the basis for needing a surrogate appointed was predetermined. The federal regulations do not appear to preclude a foster parent of a newly placed child to be appointed as a surrogate (although they do preclude a foster parent from "acting as the parent" if no ongoing, long-term relationship), as long as state-specific surrogate parent procedures are followed. Mrs. Smith's prior experience advocating for her son's education needs could certainly be evidence that she has the expertise to be such an advocate.

child. Specific procedures on who makes surrogate appointments may differ depending on state law, but often the school system is responsible for appointing surrogates.

A surrogate unknown to the child may be appointed for the child. Because at times the appointed surrogate may not know the child, and may not have any experience with the child welfare system or what it means for a child to be in foster care, this is the least desirable option. An advocate's role in this situation is to educate the surrogate on the foster care system, and the child's specific needs and situation.

How Can a Foster Parent be the Education Decision Maker?

The federal IDEA regulations state that foster parents may act as the parent, if:

- the "natural parent's authority to make educational decisions on the child's behalf has been extinguished under state law"; and

Sidebar 3

How Judges Can Help Children Receive Special Education Services

- Ask about the child's educational status:
  - Has the child been identified with a disability by the school?
  - Does the child have an IEP?
  - What services are being provided?
  - How is the child performing academically?

- Order evaluations of the child, to be conducted by professionals who are familiar with educational disabilities and the special education process.

- Order that educational records be produced for the court.

- Use a court/school liaison to assist information exchange when appropriate and speed up response and action.

- Appoint educational advocates/consultants/attorneys to pursue services for the child if none of the parties to the child welfare case are able to pursue education needs.

- Encourage the parent or the child welfare agency to obtain an educational advocate for the child.

- Receive training on special education laws and the school process.

- Use your authority to bring child welfare and school system officials together to encourage collaboration among the agencies and develop procedures that will best meet the needs of children in foster care.

- the foster parent:
  - "has an ongoing, long-term parental relationship with the child,
  - is willing to make educational decisions under the act, and
  - has no interest that would conflict with the interests of the child." [9]

This regulation raises some questions:

1. Does "act as the parent" mean that an official surrogate appointment is unnecessary when a foster parent meets the above criteria? States vary on this issue; some have foster parents appointed as surrogates and others have foster parents act as the parent (prong 3) without a formal appointment. A strict reading of the language of the regulation certainly favors the latter.

2. What does "extinguished under state law" mean? Certainly a termination of parental rights (TPR) would end the parent's rights to make educational decisions. Consult your state laws to determine if education decision-making rights of a parent of a child in foster care end before a

Special Education Websites

The Center for Law and Education
http://www.cleweb.org/
The Center works to make quality education a reality throughout the nation and to help communities address public education problems effectively. It provides expertise about the legal rights and responsibilities of students and school personnel, and key education programs, such as special education for disabled students.

Connect for Kids
http://www.connectforkids.org/
This website is for parents, educators, and policymakers who want to become more active citizens, from volunteering to voting with kids in mind. A free weekly e-letter contains information on education and disability issues.

Consortium for Appropriate Dispute Resolution in Special Education (CADRE)
http://www.directionservice.org/cadre/index.cfm
CADRE, The National Center on Dispute Resolution, is funded by the United States Department of Education, Office of Special Education Programs. CADRE uses advanced technology as well as traditional means to provide technical assistance to state departments of education on implementing mediation requirements under IDEA. CADRE also supports parents, educators and administrators to benefit from the full continuum of dispute resolution options that can prevent and resolve conflict and lead to informed partnerships that focus on results for children and youth.

The Council of Parent Attorneys and Advocates
http://www.copaa.com/
Website for attorneys, advocates, and parents to improve the quality and quantity of legal assistance for parents of children with disabilities.

FAPE Family & Advocates Partnership for Education
http://www.fape.org/
This federally funded website links families and advocates to a wealth of information about the Individuals with Disabilities Education Act (IDEA).

IDEA Practices!
http://www.ideapractices.org/
Provides news, professional development resources, and answers to questions about individuals with disabilities.

National Child Welfare Resource Center on Legal and Judicial Issues

http://www.abanet.org/child/rclji/education/home.html

The Resource Center offers a web page at its site dedicated to new developments throughout the country on education issues for children in foster care, including special education issues.

National Information Center for Children and Youth with Disabilities

http://www.nichcy.org/

Provides information about special education and related services for school children, individualized education programs, education rights, early intervention, disability and professional groups.

Office of Special Education Programs

http://www.ed.gov/offices/OSERS/OSEP/

This federal government website provides support to states and local districts to improve outcomes for infants, toddlers, children, and youth with disabilities.

Wrightslaw

http://www.wrightslaw.com/

Offers current information about special education law and advocacy for children with disabilities, parents, educators, and advocates.

Websites Addressing Specific Disabilities:

The Alexander Graham Bell Association for the Deaf and Hard of Hearing

http://www.agbell.org/

This center provides information on hearing loss and related issues, including early identification, hearing technology, and education management. Provides an extensive list of state and national resources, and information about their education advocacy program.

American Foundation for the Blind

http://www.afb.org

Provides extensive information on education issues, including IDEA and advocacy for youth who are blind.

Autism Society of America

http://www.autism-society.org/site/PageServer

Provides information on autism and pervasive developmental disorder (PDD) and treatment and educational approaches, including services under IDEA.

LDOnline

http://www.ldonline.org/

Provides online tools and information to help parents, teachers, and professionals who work with children with learning disabilities. Good source of information on both learning disabilities and attention deficit hyperactivity disorder (ADHD) issues.

National Center for Learning Disabilities

http://www.ncld.org/

Includes extensive information on all types of learning disabilities and advocacy tips for preschool and school-age children. Also includes self-advocacy information for older youth with learning disabilities.

The National Technical Assistance Consortium for Children and Young Adults Who Are Deaf-Blind

http://www.tr.wou.edu/ntac

Provides information on youth who are deaf-blind to help improve their education and transition services. Includes links to other related sites including: The National Information Clearinghouse On Children Who Are Deaf-Blind, http://www.tr.wou.edu/dblink/, and the Helen Keller National Center, http://www.helenkeller.org/national/index.htm

Special Education Publications

While these publications are not specifically about children in foster care, they are excellent sources of information about the special education process.

Capper, Lizanne. *That's My Child: Strategies for Parents of Children with Disabilities.* Washington, DC: Child Welfare League of America, Inc. 1997. Available at http://www.cwla.org ($10.95).

Cutler, Barbara. *You, Your Child, and "Special" Education. A Guide to Making the System Work.* Paul H. Brookes Publishing Co., 1993. Available at http://www.brookespublishing.com ($25.00).

Lungu, Karen. *Children with Special Needs: A Resource Guide for Parents, Educators, Social Workers & Other Caregivers.* Charles C. Thomas Publisher, 1999. Available at http://www.ccthomas.com ($38.95).

Naseef, Robert. *Special Children, Challenged Parents: The Struggles & Rewards of Raising a Child with a Disability.* Paul H. Brookes Publishing Company, 2001. Available at http://www.brookespublishing.com ($21.95).

Siegel, Lawrence. *The Complete IEP Guide: How to Advocate for Your Special Ed Child.* Nolo Press, 2001. Available at http://www.nolo.com ($17.47).

Sidebar **4** continued

Winifred, Anderson. *Negotiating the Special Education Maze: A Guide for Parents and Teachers.* Woodbine House, 1990. Available at http://woodbinehouse.com ($16.95)

Wright, Peter. *Wrightslaw: Special Education Law.* Harbor House Law Press, 1999. Available at www.wrightslaw.com ($29.95).

Wright, Peter. *Wrightslaw: From Emotions to Advocacy—The Special Education Survival Guide.* Harbor House Law Press, 1999. Available at http://www.wrightslaw.com ($24.95).

Audiovisual Materials:

The 3 R's for Special Education: Rights, Resources, Results; A Guide for Parents, A Tool for Educators
Available at http://www.pbrookes.com/store/books/trevor-6807/index.htm ($49.95) (50 min.)
This video is a resource for parents of children with disabilities and explains the choices available to meet education needs. Guardianship issues are discussed, as well as transition planning and adult services and benefits.

TPR ruling. For example, Maryland allows by statute "limited guardianship" for educational decisions to be given to the agency or an individual as early as the dispositional hearing when a parent is "unavailable, unwilling, or unable to consent to services that are in the best interest of the child."[10] If your state statute is unclear, a court may need to determine what factors to consider when deciding to strip a parent of education decision-making authority.

Another interpretation of the federal regulations could be that foster parents may "act as the parent" (prong 3) when decision making authority has been extinguished (i.e., termination of parental rights), but before that time, foster parents may be appointed as surrogates.[11]

3. What would be "an interest that would conflict with the interests of the child?" Arguably, foster parents have some emotional and monetary interest in keeping a child in their care. What if foster parents, acting as surrogate parents, had to decide if a child was to be placed in a residential setting, meaning the child would be removed from her home? Would the foster parents' emotional bond with the child, or their need for foster care payments, affect their ability to make the best decisions for the child? Or, would a foster parent, who is perhaps burned out, agree to a residential placement for a child even though the child could be maintained in the community with appropriate services? Most foster parents do have the best interests of the child at heart and would not act in their own self-interest, but this does not change the issue of the appearance of, or the potential for, conflict. (See sidebar #5 for more insight on how states handle appointing foster parents as education decision makers.)

(Note: The remainder of this chapter uses "parent" or "surrogate" to refer to the parent, guardian, person acting as the parent, or the surrogate.)

SPECIAL EDUCATION PROCESS

When Should an Eligibility Meeting Occur and What Should Happen at the Meeting to Determine Eligibility for Special Education Services?

IDEA states that the school system has a "reasonable period of time" after the evaluation request to complete the evaluations and meet as a team with the parent to determine whether the child is eligible for special education services. Many states specify a time limit for this process. For example, Maryland says this process must be completed in 90 days.[12]

IDEA specifies that the parent be entitled to a copy of any evaluation conducted by the school. While IDEA does not specify a timeframe for providing a parent a copy, advocates should ask for parents to receive copies of these evaluations before the eligibility meeting. That way, parents and surrogates can consult other professionals involved with the child to review the evaluations. Be aware, that some school psychologists will not release a report without the opportunity to review the report with the parent in person. Another reality is that often reports are not completed until right before the eligibility meeting. A parent or surrogate needs to consider whether having the evaluations in advance is worth the possible delay in holding the eligibility meeting.

If the parent or surrogate disagrees with the school's evaluation, the parent may request, in writing, an independent educational evaluation (IEE) be conducted at the school's expense. The school may either agree to this second evaluation or take the case to a due process hearing to establish whether the school's original evaluation is sufficient. (For more information on due process hearings, see discussion below).

The meeting to determine eligibility must include the parent or surrogate and a team of qualified professionals. Often the team consists of the individualized education program (IEP) team members (see discussion below). Look to your state law to determine if you have more specific requirements regarding required participants at the eligibility determination meeting. Other advocates should seek an invitation to the meeting from the parent or surrogate or the school (see further discussion below).

At the eligibility meeting, parents must be provided a copy of the written policies (known as procedural safeguards) related to their rights under IDEA. IDEA requires schools to provide these safeguards, at minimum, when the child is referred for an evaluation, when parents are notified of an IEP meeting, when the child is being reevaluated, and when the parent is registering a complaint.[13]

At this eligibility meeting, the team should review the existing evaluations, including any information provided by the parents, and any current classroom based assessments and teacher observations. Based on this information, the team must determine:

- whether the child has a disability as defined under IDEA (see definitions in sidebar #2);
- the present levels of performance and educational needs of the child;

Sample Case 3

Case #3: Carl

(Education Decision maker Role at Eligibility Meeting)

- Carl has been in foster care for two years.

- Carl's foster mother was his education decision maker ("acting as the parent") when she approached the school to evaluate Carl for a disability.

- Carl had become extremely withdrawn at home and school and his classwork and grades had been rapidly declining.

- The school psychologist evaluated Carl and determined he had suffered from depression for the past six months.

- At the eligibility meeting, one of Carl's classroom teachers started the meeting by declaring she did not think Carl had an emotional disability because she saw him laughing in the hallway last week.

What Should the Foster Parent Do?

The foster parent may want to redirect the team to the definition of "emotional disturbance" under IDEA and require the qualified evaluators to discuss Carl's eligibility in relation to the criteria in that definition. Although the school should know to follow proper steps at the eligibility team meeting, sometimes it is the education decision maker's role to keep the meeting focused on proper procedures. Some factors the team would have to examine are:

- Is Carl's depression "pervasive"?

- Has he exhibited this for a "long period of time" and "to a marked degree"?

- Has this condition adversely affected Carl's educational performance?

- How have these issues impacted on school performance?

- whether the child needs special education and related services (i.e., whether the child is able to make "meaningful education progress" without intervention).

Your role as an advocate for the child is to participate in the process as much as possible to ensure these IDEA-dictated procedures are being followed. For example, are the right individuals present? Have procedural safeguards been provided? Has the parent or surrogate reviewed the procedural safeguards and do they understand them? Are evaluations appropriate and being reviewed? Is the eligibility decision truly a team decision? Bring a copy of the IDEA definitions (and a list from your state code or regulation if they differ) and ensure that the team is using the criteria outlined in the definition of each disability.

Foster Parents as the Education Advocate

The role that foster parents can play for children in foster care who have, or are suspected of having, disabilities, can be confusing. In different states and jurisdictions, the appointment and procedures involving foster parents vary widely. Some states appoint them as surrogate parents. Some allow foster parents to act as the parent without such appointment, while others do not allow foster parents to be the education advocate for the child. We spoke with two foster parents who have served as the education decision maker for children in the foster care system. These are just two of many examples of how states determine who is the education decision maker for a child in foster care.

North Dakota Foster Parent

The first caretaker has been a foster parent for about 27 years, and has had approximately 20 children in her care over that time. In addition, she and her husband have three biological children, who are all adults now.

Q: How did you learn about becoming an education decision maker?

A: I have a master's degree in education and was a teacher for 20 years before I resigned. When I started teaching, there were always children in my classroom I wanted to bring home who needed extra care. I have always fought for children whose parents didn't know what to fight for or didn't know what services the children could be getting.

I knew about children in care needing education advocates when I was a teacher, but took on that role officially when I became a foster parent.

Q: What special needs did the children in your care have?

A: We have had children with all sorts of disabilities and special needs. We have had children with emotional disturbances, cerebral palsy and many other disabilities. We had one child with a significant brain disease that impacted his ability to speak. These disabilities strongly impacted their ability to succeed in school.

Q: How important is it for children to have an advocate for their educational needs?

A: I believe that every child deserves and has the right to an education. Sometimes we don't expect enough from children with disabilities. Schoolwork will be simplified for them and the expectation level of professionals will not be as high as it would be for nondisabled students. By the same token, the work may end up being too difficult for the developmental level of a child. The reasons for this can vary; for example, it may be that the child's records weren't available at the time the child entered the new school, interfering with good education planning for the child. It is important that we treat children with disabilities as much like their nondisabled peers as is reasonable and appropriate. A child's advocate can ensure that the child is getting fair treatment and that the child is learning and making academic strides.

Q: What obstacles are there in your state to foster parents being the education decision maker?

A: There is a tremendous lack of understanding about who has education decision-making authority for children when they are in foster care. Schools are confused about this issue, but so are child welfare caseworkers. Often, caseworkers think they have the authority and will sign IEPs. Schools also think this is appropriate. Because of my education background, and my interest in getting the right services for the children in my care, I always go to meetings and act in the role of the parent. But I have never been officially appointed as a surrogate parent. There needs to be a lot more education in this arena to provide the consistency that is so necessary.

Q: What do you do in your role as education decision maker?

A: I believe that my job is to look out for the educational interests of the child, and to be a voice for that child. When I know a child is going to be placed in my home, I go to the school before the child is placed to start talking with the school. I also try to get the educational records before the child arrives. I will often meet with the principal and/or counselor personally to discuss any issues. I want to ensure that the first day will go smoothly.

I also attend all meetings for the child, and will call meetings at any point if things are not going as agreed. For example, if at an IEP meeting the teacher agreed to provide the student with highlighted textbooks, and if the child comes home the next day without the highlighted text books, I will call the school, and follow up in writing, to explain that the textbooks were not brought home. I will put in the letter that if the books are not brought home the next day that I will call the school the following morning to inquire about them. The best advocates do not allow grass to grow under their feet.

Q: Why are foster parents uniquely qualified to be the child's education decision maker?

A: Because we know the child's strengths and weaknesses better than anyone. We spend so many hours with these children. We know if the child has self esteem issues, or psychological issues, or problems seeing or hearing. I read with every child in my home. I know within a short time of the child entering my home whether the child is struggling with sight words or is having other reading difficulties. It often takes time for children to open up in school. Because the home setting is less formal and more intimate, children tend to open up faster at home.

Q: Have you ever been involved as the education decision maker when the birth parents were also involved with the educational decision of the child and attended school meetings?

A: Yes. In those situations I think that my role is to help teach the parents how to take the lead and advocate for their child. In one case that I can remember, the parents were the ones who signed the IEP, but the school had the caseworker and I sign as well. Although only the parent's signature was required, this approach showed the child that everyone involved in his life was in agreement as to his plan, which was important.

Q: Have you had any formal training in education advocacy?

A: No. Everything I have learned has been self-taught. My background in education has helped a lot. I take advantage of every book, website, and publication out there dealing with children with special needs. I make it a point to take time to learn about the unique needs of every child in my home. If I can't talk the talk, I can't walk the walk. I often tell children who come into my home that I will support you and do everything I can for you, the same as I do for my birth children. I would not be able to keep that promise if I did not educate myself to be the best advocate for them that I can be.

North Carolina Foster Parent

This caretaker has been a foster parent for the past five years, and has had seven children in her care over that period. She has had a long career working with adults with disabilities and special needs. For the past three years she has worked at a nonprofit which provides technical assistance to parents and foster parents on special education issues for children with disabilities. The nonprofit also is responsible for training and providing the volunteers to be appointed as surrogate parents by the school system for children that need them. It has a small grant from the child welfare agency to provide this assistance to foster parents.

Q: How did you learn about becoming an education decision maker?

A: I have spent years working with adults with disabilities so I have a lot of understanding of disability issues. In the last three years I have worked with children with disabilities and been trained to be a surrogate. In addition to "acting as the parent" to make education decisions for some of the children in my home, I have also been formally appointed a surrogate for other children in foster care who are not in my care.

Q: What is the importance of children having an advocate for their education needs?

A: It is very important that a child has an advocate to initiate evaluations if a child is struggling and no one has considered special education needs. Advocates also play an important role watching a child's progress and making sure appropriate follow up is made.

Q: What obstacles are there in your state to having foster parents be the education decision maker for a child in foster care?

A: In our jurisdiction, foster parents are considered to be the "parent" if the plan for the child has changed from reunification. There is no need for that foster parent to be appointed as a surrogate or go through any of the surrogate requirements. Surrogates will be appointed when children are in group homes, therapeutic foster homes, hospitals or in foster homes where the foster parent does not feel qualified to act as the surrogate. One big obstacle is that therapeutic foster parents are not permitted to be surrogates in many jurisdictions. For some reason they are considered an "agency caring for the child" where regular foster parents are not. It is a real difficulty, because the children in therapeutic foster care are often those that have the most significant special education needs.

Also, we have difficulties getting surrogates appointed for our infants and toddlers in the child welfare system. Often we are told that these young children don't need surrogates, even though IDEA says they do.

A third obstacle is that our surrogate pool has dwindled. We need to get more volunteers. I have been thinking about doing a public interest article in the local paper about the program and why it is so important for children in the hopes of interesting new volunteers.

Q: What do you do in your education decision maker role?

A: I currently do not have any foster children in my home. However, I am appointed as a surrogate for a 17-year-old boy who is placed in a group home in our area. He is diagnosed with mental retardation, and other than the first five years of his life when he lived with his mother, he has been living in institutions. He was moved to the group home last February, and in March they wanted to transition him to the public school for the first time in his life. I have been pushing for thorough evaluations to be conducted to determine his skill levels and abilities, as well as trying to advocate for a more gradual transition into a regular school setting. To place this child into a public school without the right supports in place will just set him up to fail.

Q: Why are foster parents uniquely qualified to be the child's education decision maker?

A: They end up knowing the child the best. They know the skills and abilities of the child in their care. They often are in the best position to create a strength-based plan. However, I need to point out that not all foster parents want to, or should be, education decision makers for the children in their care. Sometimes someone from our trained pool of surrogates may be better suited to play that role. You really need to look at each child's situation and determine what is best on a case-by-case basis.

Q: Have you ever been involved as the education decision maker when the birth parents were also involved with the educational decision of the child and attended school meetings?

A: Yes, I had a child in my care whose plan was reunification with her father. While she was in my care both her father and I went to IEP meetings, but the father was the official decision maker and signed the appropriate documents. I was able to provide input and information for the father and the team, and my role was a valuable one.

Q: Have you had any formal training as an education decision maker?

A: Yes. I went through the formal surrogate parent training at my organization when I first started…and now I train other people to be surrogate parents. I try to take advantage of as many outside special education trainings as I can. I've been to some state and national conferences on this topic.

Who is Part of the Individualized Education Program (IEP) Team?

Once eligibility has been determined, an IEP must be developed. The IEP team develops and revises the IEPs, and often is the same team that makes decisions about eligibility. Federal law requires that the IEP team include:

- parents
- regular education teacher
- special education teacher
- school system representative who is qualified to provide instruction for children with disabilities, and knows about the general curriculum and the avail-

ability of resources (e.g., principal, vice principal, school administrator)

- an individual who can interpret the instructional implications of evaluation results (e.g., school psychologist, speech and language therapist)
- at the discretion of the parent or the school system, other individuals with knowledge or expertise about the child, including related services personnel
- the child, if appropriate.[14]

If you, as the advocate, are the parent or surrogate, then you are part of the IEP team. However, what about other advo-

Sidebar *5* continued

Q: Do GALs ever get involved in these education matters?

A: Occasionally they do. I have conducted surrogate parent trainings for the GALs. I often expect the GALs to be more knowledgeable than the foster parents on special education issues, but in reality they often do not know about IDEA and the legal protections that exist. One of the biggest issues we see is that no one is initiating the special education process by referring for evaluations. I believe that in addition to foster parents, GALs could be instrumental in making sure these referrals are happening.

Q: What advice do you have for children's representatives on involvement in education matters?

A: One criticism I hear is that surrogates don't really get to know the child's needs or take time to observe them in the school setting. If there is a parent who just can't attend meetings because of incarceration, then I think the surrogate needs to try to contact the parent to see what their educational desires would be and to bring those to the table. Educational advocacy can be difficult and so it is important to attend additional workshops about IDEA and parents' rights and responsibilities. I believe it is also important to know other agencies working on educational advocacy issues to call when you have a question or need to involve another expert. One expert can't know about all disabilities and every educational strategy, but advocacy is the same for any disability. We all need to work together to help children reach their full potential, which is different for every child.

cates not appointed to that role? The school must invite a representative of any other agency that is likely to be responsible for providing or paying for transition services when transition planning is being discussed at an IEP meeting (which must happen by the child's 14th birthday, if not sooner).[15] This will likely mean that child welfare agency personnel must be included in these IEP meetings for older youth (more on transition planning below).

Best practice would dictate that any child welfare advocates who have contact with the child and play a role in the child's life be included in IEP meetings. Participating at the IEP meeting is possible through two avenues: the discretion of the parent (or surrogate parent) or the discretion of the school system. When the parent is still making educational decisions, and the parent has a good relationship with you, the parent may request your presence at the IEP meeting. Likewise, if the parent surrogate knows about the child welfare case, it is likely the surrogate would invite the other child advocates to the school meetings.

Problems arise when there is either an uncooperative parent who still retains education decision-making rights, or a surrogate parent who is unaware of, or uninterested in involving, child welfare advocates. A solution to both situations is to be invited to the team by the school. You may need to establish a relationship with school personnel, and convince them that your presence at the IEP team meetings is necessary to achieve good educational planning for the child. In this way, even if you lack legal decision-making authority, you can still play a role advocating for the child's educational needs.

What is an Individualized Education Program (IEP) and How Should it Be Developed?

Once a child is found in need of special education services, IDEA requires that an IEP be developed within 30 days.[16] An IEP is a written plan outlining the child's needs and how the school must address those needs. It must be detailed and child specific, and when implemented, should result in the child making meaningful educational progress. When the parent or surrogate signs the IEP, she agrees to everything it contains.

The IEP must be developed with input from all team members, including the parent or surrogate. Be wary when an IEP is prepared before an IEP meeting and merely presented to the parent or surrogate for signature. This is not to say that school staff cannot suggest some provisions for the IEP, as long as they are presented to the parent or surrogate in that manner, explained fully, and there are opportunities for the parent or surrogate to comment on the provisions and discuss and add or delete provisions as necessary.

Key IEP elements include:

- **The child's present levels of educational performance:** This information is needed to measure how much progress a child is making as a result of the IEP services.

- **Measurable annual goals, including benchmarks or short-term objectives:** This section spells out reasonable expectations for progress for the child in the coming year. In the IEP document, the team specifies broad educational goals for the child, with more specific short-term objectives. For example, a broad goal could be improving written language, while the short-term objective could be "given a topic, write a persuasive paragraph." These goals and objectives must be measurable (e.g., by evaluations, reviewing student work, or observation) and must specify what level of mastery is expected (e.g., 80% accuracy). The goals must also specify who is responsible for monitoring this progress (e.g., classroom teacher).

- **The special education and related services and supplementary aids and services, program modifications, and staff supports to be provided:** Based on the goals and objectives established for the child, the team then determines what services will help the child achieve these goals. These include any related services (See sidebar #6 for examples of related services). The IEP must specify when the services will begin, and the anticipated frequency, location, and duration of the services and modifications. For example, a child may receive one hour per day, five days a week of specialized instruction in a special education classroom to work on writing skills. The child may also need one hour per week of occupational therapy as a related service.

- **Statement of transition services:** This portion of the IEP requires:
  - **By age 14:** The team must address what instruction will assist the child prepare for transition.[17]

Sample Case 4

Case #4: Dawn
(Developing a Statement of Transition Services)

- Dawn is 16 and has a speech and language disability in addition to an emotional disability due to serious depression.

- Dawn has had an IEP for four years.

- Two years ago, Dawn's IEP team discussed the need for a statement of transition services as part of Dawn's IEP. Dawn's IEP mentions that Dawn will attend a career fair at school.

What should an advocate do?

- Talk with Dawn and help her discover her interests, including education goals.

- Request an immediate IEP meeting to discuss transition planning and develop a detailed statement of transition services.

- Consider requesting a vocational assessment, if more information is needed to determine Dawn's skill level, interests, and so forth.

- Instruct Dawn's English teacher to select books and writing assignments for Dawn that will expose her to employment-related topics.

- Ensure Dawn's speech therapist, who meets with Dawn three times a week, works with Dawn on developing vocabulary and understanding language associated with employment, resumes, and job interviewing.

- In the statement of transition services, include Dawn's need for a job coach for Dawn's first job or a provision that Dawn may shadow others in careers she is considering until she decides which career she will pursue. Also include services related to researching, applying, and interviewing for continued and higher education programs.

- Encourage Dawn to take part in a school/work program.

- **By age 16:** The IEP must state what transition services the child needs, and specify interagency responsibilities or needed linkages.[18]

Be aware of the kinds of transition services available under IDEA for a child with a disability. (See sidebar #6 for transition services that can be offered under IDEA.)

All child welfare advocates need to ensure the transition planning happening as part of a child's IEP is coordinated with the youth's transition planning in the child welfare system.

- **Whether the child qualifies for extended school year (ESY) services:** Qualifying for ESY services depends on several factors, among them: whether a child with a disability would regress significantly over the summer break, and how much time it will take a child to regain skills learned the previous year.[19] If a child qualifies, the child is entitled to school services over the summer.

- **The recommended placement for the child:** The team must determine where the services will be provided. There is a continuum of placement options, from a regular education classroom with minimal supports to a residential treatment facility. The services identified in the IEP must be provided in the least restrictive environment (LRE). In some cases, the local school may not be able to recommend a placement, other than specify that it cannot provide the services. In these cases, the placement decision may occur at a separate meeting involving additional school system officials, and sometimes at a central school system office.

How Should I Prepare for an IEP Meeting?
Before the meeting
- Think about what you would like to see the child accomplish in the coming year. Consider listing the child's strengths, needs, and interests and your major concerns about his education.[20]
- Collect and bring any documentation describing the child's disability, behaviors, and school progress (e.g., evaluations, child's schoolwork examples).
- Review materials you have collected and any materials the school has sent you. If the school has not given you any advance materials, request a copy of the record that will be discussed at the meeting. Review the evaluations and

determine if you agree with the conclusions, or if the described behavior in the evaluation matches what you know of the child.
- If you are an attorney, make sure you notify the school that you will be attending the meeting. The school will then have the right to have a school attorney present at the meeting.

At the meeting
- **Participating at the meeting:** Share your knowledge about the child and carefully listen to what others say about the child to be able to respond appropriately. If you do not understand something, ask for clarification.
- **Tape recording:** In many states, parents and their advocates have a right to tape record IEP meetings, as long as they notify the school beforehand and the school allows the meeting to be taped. Frequently, the school will record the meeting as well. Since many people attend these meetings, much information is given orally and conversations are often intense. Therefore, taping is a great way to document everything said by the team.
- **Signing the IEP:** If you are the parent or the surrogate, and are asked at the end of the meeting to sign the IEP consenting to everything it contains, be sure you understand fully what you are being asked to approve. You are permitted to delay signing for a reasonable period, to take the document home to review outside of the sometimes pressure-filled meeting room, or to consult with other professionals involved with the child. If the parent or surrogate does not agree with the IEP, she should not sign. Note that if this is the initial IEP, services can-

not begin for the child until the IEP is signed. If this is a revised IEP, the school must provide services according to the old IEP until a new IEP is agreed to and signed.

- **Copies and follow up:** Make sure you are given a copy of the notes and all documents from the meeting. If anyone at the meeting has promised to provide additional information to you, be sure to follow up with that team member, preferably in writing.

MONITORING AND IMPLEMENTATION
What Do I Do if I Suspect a Child is Identified with the Wrong Disability?

It is critical that a child receiving special education services be correctly identified with the appropriate disability. Keep in mind that a child's identified disability will guide the services the school arranges for that child. However, once identified to receive special education services, the child will be eligible to receive any services the IEP team finds are needed.[21]

You may encounter cases where a child in foster care already has an IEP, but upon reviewing the information in that document it becomes clear, or you suspect, that the child's disability has been misidentified and the child has other needs not addressed in the IEP. In these cases, additional services can be added by the IEP team without further evaluations, however you may still want to make a written request to the school system for a meeting either to review the IEP or to reevaluate the child's disability. This is also true for a child who may have multiple disabilities, but has only been identified with one.

If you feel a child who is receiving special education services may not need those services, request an IEP meeting to reevaluate the child. If the reevaluation finds the child does not have, or no longer has, a disability, the child will be discharged from special education.

How Should I Monitor the Student's Progress and the Implementation of the IEP?

- After an IEP is in place, monitor how the services are working for the child. Review assignments and tests that the child brings home.
- Find out what the child thinks about the new services, whether they are helpful, and what, if anything, needs to be changed.
- Communicate regularly with the child's teachers through phone calls, e-mails, or progress reports.
- A parent or surrogate can request an IEP meeting any time if there is reason to believe the IEP is not being implemented appropriately or if something needs to be added or changed. At a minimum, IDEA requires an annual review of the IEP to review achievement of past goals and establish goals and services for the coming year.
- IDEA requires that a child with a disability be reevaluated at least every three years.[22] However, it also states that a reevaluation shall be conducted whenever conditions warrant, or if the child's parent or teacher requests one.[23] Parents and surrogates should not hesitate to request a reevaluation of a child if they feel it is warranted.
- Discharge from special education: IDEA provides that the school system cannot decide that a child is no longer eligible

Examples of Services that Can Be Provided Under IDEA

RELATED SERVICES "means transportation and such developmental, corrective, and other supportive services as are required to assist a child with a disability to benefit from special education, and includes speech-language pathology and audiology services, psychological services, physical and occupational therapy, recreation, including therapeutic recreation, early identification and assessment of disabilities in children, counseling services, including rehabilitation counseling, orientation and mobility services, and medical services for diagnostic or evaluation purposes. The term also includes school health services, social work services in schools, and parent counseling and training." 34 C.F.R. § 300.24(a)

TRANSITION SERVICES means a coordinated set of activities for a student with a disability that—

(A) is designed within an outcome-oriented process, which promotes movement from school to post-school activities, including post-secondary education, vocational training, integrated employment (including supported employment), continuing and adult education, adult services, independent living, or community participation;

(B) is based upon the individual student's needs, taking into account the student's preferences and interests; and

(C) includes instruction, related services, community experiences, the development of employment and other post-school adult living objectives, and, when appropriate, acquisition of daily living skills and functional vocational evaluation. 20 U.S.C. § 1401(30); 34 C.F.R. § 300.29

for special education services without first evaluating the child.[24] This protects the child from being terminated from special education erroneously, and requires that termination be based on a thorough evaluation of the child.

What If I Do Not Agree with the Decision Reached by the IEP Team?

If the parent or surrogate does not agree with the decisions made by the team regarding identification, services, or placement, she should not sign the IEP. The parent or surrogate has three options: mediation, due process hearing, and state board of education complaints.

Mediation and/or a due process hearing should be seen as the last straw in advocating the needs of the child. For example, if an IEP meeting has gotten heated, an interim strategy may be to reconvene the meeting in a few days to see if resolution can be reached short of mediation and due process. At times, mediation and/or a due process hearing may be needed.

Mediation must be provided, at a minimum, whenever a due process hearing is requested. Often states permit mediation to be requested without scheduling a due process hearing. Mediation is voluntary and cannot be used to deny or delay a parent's right to a hearing. A qualified and impartial mediator must conduct the mediation, and the school bears the cost of the mediation. All information shared in mediation is confidential and cannot be used in a later due process hearing. If agreement can be reached during mediation, the terms of the agreement must be documented in writing.

A **due process hearing** is a trial-like administrative proceeding, where evidence and witnesses are presented and cross-examined. A hearing officer presides over the hearing and issues a written ruling in the case. A successful result at a due process hearing may involve obtaining appropriate services or placement for a child, and also can involve receiving compensatory services (services to make up for the school's error or failures) and money to recoup costs and attorney expenses.

Due process hearings can be complicated. If you do not have experience pursuing these kinds of hearings, proceed with caution. Parents and surrogate parents may appear unrepresented, however that is often unwise, as these hearings can involve long and intense conflicts. School systems are frequently represented by attorneys with expertise in this area of law. An attorney without experience handling due process cases should ask an experienced

education attorney for assistance, to co-counsel, or even handle the case.

Another method of noting a disagreement is to file an **IDEA complaint with your state** department of education. The advantages of this type of complaint over a due process proceeding are that it is less time intensive and stressful, and it resolves issues in a less adversarial manner. This type of complaint can be effective for procedural violations or clear-cut issues (e.g., Were the appropriate team members present at the child's IEP meeting?). Problems with this type of complaint are that states vary in the quality of their investigations and decision making, and this method may not effectively resolve quality issues (e.g., Is this speech language therapy adequately meeting the child's needs?).

CONCLUSION

You can help link children in foster care to special education services and ensure those services are meeting their needs. Understanding the IDEA and what services are available to children in the foster care system is critical to navigating the special education process. With child welfare systems struggling to provide all children in care with the services they need, failing to access services under IDEA is wasting an important source of education assistance for these children.

Endnotes

[1] Van Wingerden, Claire, John Emerson, and Dennis Ichikawa. "Improving Special Education for Children with Disabilities in Foster Care." *Casey Family Programs, Foundations for the Future: Education Brief. Education Issue Brief: Improving Special Education for Children with Disabilities in Foster Care.* Seattle, Washington: Casey Family Programs, June 2002.

[2] See chapter 2 for more information about basic legal rights under IDEA and other federal laws related to education.

[3] The reason the evaluation would not be at the school's expense is because of the strategic decision to pursue the evaluation without involving the school system. Schools would be responsible for the expense of the evaluation if they were requested to conduct the evaluation, or an additional independent educational evaluation (IEE).

[4] 20 U.S.C. § 1415(b)(2).

[5] Ibid.

[6] 34 C.F.R. § 300.20(a).

[7] 34 C.F.R. § 300.515(c)(2)(i).

[8] E.g., see Cal. Gov. Code § 7579.5: When appointing a surrogate parent, the local educational agency shall, as a first preference, select a relative caretaker, foster parent, or court-appointed special advocate, if any of these individuals exists and is willing and able to serve.

[9] 34 C.F.R. § 300.20.

[10] Md. Code Ann., Courts and Judicial Proceedings § 3-819(c)1(ii) (Supp. 2003).

[11] E.g., see Nevada Department of Education. "The Appointment of Surrogate Parents for Students with Disabilities." February 2000.

[12] Md. Regs. Code § 13A.05.01.06A.

[13] 20 U.S.C. § 1415(d).

[14] 34 C.F.R. § 300.344.

[15] 34 C.F.R. §300.344(b)(3).

[16] 34 C.F.R. § 300.343 (b)(2).

[17] 34 C.F.R. §300.347(b)(1)(i).

[18] 34 C.F.R. §300.347(b)(2).

[19] For an in-depth discussion of ESY, see Margolis, Leslie Seid. *Extended School Year Services Under IDEA*. Washington, DC: National Association of Protection and Advocacy Systems, Inc. Available for purchase from http://www.napas.org/I-6/pub%20awareness%20mat%20home.htm.

[20] For more information on planning for an IEP meeting, see *Planning Your Child's Individualized Education Program: Some Suggestions to Consider*. Minneapolis, MN: Families and Advocates Partnership for Education, Pacer Center Inc., Sept. 2001. < http://www.fape.org/pubs/FAPE-25%20Planning%20Your%20Childs%20IEP.pdf>

[21] This means that if a child is identified with a learning disability and also has some behavior problems, even though the behaviors don't rise to the level of an additional educational disability identification, the child's IEP can include goals and objectives or services to address the behavior issues.

[22] 20 U.S.C. § 1414 (a)(2).

[23] 20 U.S.C. § 1414(a)(2)(A).

[24] 20 U.S.C. § 1414 (c)(5); 34 C.F.R. § 300.534 (c)(1).

4

MEETING THE EDUCATION NEEDS
OF YOUNG CHILDREN

INTRODUCTION

Children under five make up 40% of all children entering foster care; 25% of those are children under two, and 20% are children under one.[1] Knowing how to advocate for a young child's education and development needs is part of your job as a child welfare professional. However, it is the area where most advocates struggle.

Some overlook education issues for young children because they are not yet in school. This thinking may be based on a narrow definition of education. Education, as it relates to children from birth through age five, encompasses health, growth, and development. Research shows these early years are critical for developing and acquiring social/emotional as well as language and cognitive skills that are key to future academic success.[2] Other studies show that early literacy skills predict later school success.[3]

This chapter helps you understand the education needs of young children who have entered foster care. You'll receive tips on navigating and advocating for services and programs that help ensure healthy development and a successful educational future.

WHAT THE RESEARCH SHOWS
Impact of Abuse and Neglect on Young Children

Many young children in foster care have been directly exposed to neglect, maltreatment, family or community violence, or exposed prenatally to drugs or alcohol, to name a few possible factors. Research shows these experiences can have the following consequences for young children in foster care:

- maltreatment: compromised physical, cognitive, emotional, and social development in later childhood and adulthood.[4]
- parental neglect and physical abuse: social withdrawal, inattentiveness, and cognitive underachievement in elementary school.[5]
- Fetal Alcohol Spectrum Disorders: birth defects, resulting in developmental delays, speech and language problems, attention deficits, impulsive and hyperactive behavior, growth problems, cardiac abnormalities, and mental retardation.[6]
- caregiver separation/multiple placements: grief, rage, attachment difficulties, mental health problems (post traumatic stress disorder, regulatory disorders, attachment disorders, depressive disorders, and anxiety disorders).[7]

(For more detail about these studies and other important research see sidebar #5).

ADDRESSING NEEDS: KEY PROGRAMS

The more resources devoted to young children, the more likely they will not suffer the lasting effects of their early experiences. Statistics show the very youngest children (under three months old when entering care)

spend the longest time in foster care.[8] More focus on education and services for this young population could result in shorter stays in foster care and more permanent placements. Additionally, quality care and education services can avoid future abuse and neglect. It is not enough to know about the needs and issues that young children in foster care face. Child welfare advocates need to ensure appropriate services are provided and the needs of young children are met.

Young children may be eligible for a variety of programs and services designed to promote healthy development and early education success. This section highlights four key programs advocates should always explore when working with a young child.

EPSDT

Healthy child development early in life paves the road for educational success. One federal program available for virtually all young children in foster care is Early and Periodic Screening, Diagnosis, and Treatment (EPSDT).[9] EPSDT is a comprehensive and preventive child health program that is part of Medicaid. All individuals who are eligible for Medicaid and under age 21 are also eligible for EPSDT services. EPSDT requires regular and periodic physical, hearing, vision, and dental exams.

Children should be scheduled for an EPSDT physical exam at regular intervals from birth to 21. These intervals need to be frequent during the first 18 months of life. Dental services require a referral and must be provided according to a schedule that meets reasonable standards of dental practice and at any other time a dental referral is medically necessary.

EPSDT services include immunizations, blood and urine tests, child development exams, nutritional evaluations, preventive and restorative dental care, eyeglasses, hearing aids, durable medical equipment, home health care, help with transportation and scheduling, and any additional medically necessary services prescribed by the exams, even those services not covered in a state's Medicaid plan.[10]

Practice Tips:

- Ensure eligible children are enrolled in the EPSDT program by their primary care doctor (listed on their Medicaid card).
- To confirm that a child is eligible for Medicaid, contact your local department of human services or social services, health department, or Medicaid regional office. For more information, visit http://www.cms.hhs.gov/medicaid/consumerfam.asp.
- Make sure young children have a "medical home" where they are seen regularly by a treating physician who knows their medical history and ensures they receive all needed evaluations, treatment, and follow up.
- Educate yourself on healthy development and point out resources available on child development to the child's caretaker and/or caseworker to improve their understanding of healthy development and enable them to look for signs of problems (see sidebars #1 for resources and #6 for a checklist on developmental milestones).
- Make sure parents are informed of medical information, diagnosis, and treatment and consulted about the child's medical history.

Quality Care and Education Settings

Quality care and education for young children begins at home. Advocates need to pay attention to how knowledgeable the child's care provider is about the child's needs and development. This is true regardless of the permanency plan, and any care providers—be they the parent, foster parent, relative caretaker, or adoptive parent—must know or be educated on the needs of young children.

Care and education of young children also occurs outside the home. It is an increasing reality that working families, foster families, and relative caretakers struggle to find affordable, quality care for their young children. Traditional child care facilities often lack standards and training to adequately meet young children's unique needs.

It is not enough for advocates to know a child is in "day care." Factors to look for in early care and education programs that signal an appropriate setting include:

- a safe facility, equipped with appropriate toys and materials;
- well-trained, educated, and compensated teachers and staff;
- small class size and low adult-child ratios;
- positive relationships between teachers and children that include communication throughout the day, both listening and responding and encouragement for reasoning and problem solving;
- emphasis on social and learning skills;
- exposure to an array of activities and experiences, including art, music, science, math and different kinds of play; and involvement of parents or caretakers.[11]

Internet Resources for Young Children

Early Care and Education Collaborative
http://www.earlycare.org/

Head Start
http://www.nhsa.org/index.htm

Miami Safe Start Initiative
http://www.miamisafestart.org/

National Association for the Education of Young Children
http://www.naeyc.org/

National Early Childhood Technical Assistance Center
http:www.nectac.org/

National Institute for Early Education Research
http://nieer.org/

New York Permanent Judicial Commission on Justice for Children
http://www.courts.state.ny.us/ip/justiceforchildren/index.shtml

Zero to Three
http://www.zerotothree.org/
Information on child development: http://www.zerotothree.org/healthyminds/
Information on school readiness: http://www.zerotothree.org/ztt_parentAZ.html

While these factors are the characteristics that all parents look for in care settings for young children, a quality setting is even more critical for a child in foster care. As a result of their possible exposure to multiple risk factors, these young children may have additional needs and behaviors that must be addressed appropriately. The factors and tips discussed in this section are not exhaustive. They offer a starting point for finding appropriate, quality care and education for young children in care.

Practice Tips:
- Learn about the range of available care and education programs in your community. Contact your child welfare agency for a list of providers.
- Try to match the needs of each young child to the most appropriate program.
- Investigate placement options for young children. Can the program address the child's needs?
- Know details about the care and education young children are receiving. Ensure that factors necessary to meet their needs exist in that setting.

Head Start and Early Head Start

Two federally supported early care and education programs exist in every state with the components to aid young children in care and meet their needs—Head Start and Early Head Start.

Head Start

Head Start is a comprehensive early health and education program for children age three to five years from low-income families. Head Start programs help children develop social, emotional, and cognitive skills. Children can receive a variety of health care services such as immunizations, dental, medical, nutritional, and mental health services through the Head Start program. Head Start also encourages caregivers to be active in their children's education by volunteering and planning activities in the classroom as well as by attending workshops on child-related topics. Families can also access other social services such as job counseling through their child's Head Start program. While many Head Start programs offer full-day programs, some are only partial day.

To be eligible for Head Start, family income usually must meet the federal poverty income guidelines. Ten percent of the spaces in a Head Start program must be used for children with disabilities. Some states have provisions that make children in foster care a priority for enrollment. However, the reality in many jurisdictions is that there are not enough Head Start programs to accommodate all eligible children, including children in foster care.

Early Head Start

Early Head Start was created in 1994 to promote school success by helping the physical, emotional, social, and intellectual development of low-income children from birth to age three. Early Head Start also serves low-income pregnant women.

Early Head Start programs can be home-based, center-based, home and center-based, or locally designed. Early Head Start provides a variety of parent education services including home visits and peer support groups. Pregnant women also receive comprehensive health services, including prenatal and postpartum health care, mental health interventions, and breastfeeding information. Children receive health screenings, dental screenings, and other medical services for conditions such as asthma, anemia, developmental disabilities and delays, behavioral problems, and vision and hearing problems. In addition, many Early Head Start programs provide child care services by partnering with local child care centers. Early Head Start programs also coordinate their services with local Head Start programs to ensure continuity of services as children grow.

Practice Tips:

- Determine if you can enroll a child into a Head Start or Early Head Start by contacting the local Head Start agency serving your community. To locate a local Head Start program in your area, access the online national Head Start Program Search Tool at: http://www.acf.hhs.gov/programs/hsb/hs web/index.jsp or call the Head Start Information and Publication Center, 866/763-6481.

- Be sure to ask if children in foster care are given special consideration for enrollment.

- Determine the extent of services and care provided by the Head Start or Early Head Start program. For example, if it is only a partial day program what are the child's other care options?

Individuals with Disabilities Education Act (IDEA)

Many children in the foster care system between birth and age five may be eligible for services under IDEA. Children between birth and age three who qualify under IDEA are eligible under Part C and children ages three through five who qualify are eligible under Part B.

Part C

Before 1986, only children over age three could be eligible for services under the Individuals with Disabilities Education Act (IDEA). When IDEA was amended in 1986, a provision was added providing services to children from birth through age three who had disabilities or were suspected of having disabilities. This provision is known as Part C of the IDEA.

The referral, evaluation, and eligibility process for accessing services under Part C is similar to the process for accessing services for children age three through 21 under Part B of the IDEA. (See chapter 3 for information about the eligibility process under Part B of IDEA, and sidebar #2 for a chart highlighting the differences between Part C and Part B). Key elements include:

Referral. A referral must be made to the entity responsible for Part C services in your state. In many states, that will be the Department of Education, so start there. If the Department of Education does not provide Part C services in your state, it can refer you to the appropriate agency to make your request. Most states allow anyone to make the referral.

Required Part C referrals for substantiated cases. A new provision regarding Part C referrals can be found in the recent reauthorization of the Child Abuse Prevention and Treatment Act (CAPTA). Signed into law in July 2003, CAPTA now *requires* states to have procedures in place for child welfare caseworkers to make referrals for early intervention services for children from birth to age three for *all* substantiated abuse and neglect cases.[12] This requirement is substantial in that it not only requires referral procedures for cases that have been petitioned in dependency court, it also requires referral procedures for those cases that have administrative findings of substantiated abuse or neglect, but no court involvement.

Frontline investigative caseworkers need to be informed about this requirement and trained on the IDEA Part C process and services. Note that this heightened referral requirement does not guarantee that all children referred will receive Part C services. It requires that the process to evaluate and screen the child be initiated to determine whether those services are warranted.

Evaluation. After you have referred the child, the responsible entity must arrange a developmental assessment or evaluation. This Part C assessment is not just of the child (as it is under Part B), but the entire family. Healthy development of young children with developmental issues can only be ensured if families receive training and support to help nurture them. Foster families and birth families can be involved in this evaluation, depending on the circumstances of the case. Once a referral is received, the entity has 45 days to complete the evaluation and assessment and hold a meeting.[13]

Parent/surrogate parent appointment. Defining parent under the IDEA, and appointing surrogate parents in certain circumstances is an important component of the IDEA under Part B and Part C. Advocates must understand how the term parent is defined, under what circumstances foster parents and other caregivers are permitted to act as the parent, and how and when surrogates are appointed. (For an in-depth discussion of the federal statute and regulations related to parent surrogates see sidebar #3.) Be sure to consult your state statutes and regulations, since the way states apply these provisions differ. Note that a parent or surrogate of a child eligible under Part C determines whether the child will access these needed services (see further discussion of parent refusal below).

Service coordinator. The Part C entity must appoint a service coordinator for the family early in the process. This service coordinator acts as a case manager throughout the process and coordinates all needed services for the child and family. The appointment of a service coordinator early in the process is especially important for children in foster care, as coordination may be needed among numerous parties, namely parents, child welfare agency staff, and foster parents.

IFSP team members. The parent or surrogate, the service coordinator, and the evaluator are required to attend an eligibility and individualized family service plan (IFSP) development meeting. Others may be included. For children in foster care, other individuals with information about the young child, such as caseworkers, child attorneys, guardians ad litem, and other advocates, should be included (see Chapter 3 regarding getting invited to team meetings.)

Eligibility. Part C requires states to provide services to young children in two categories:

- **Children diagnosed with a mental or physical condition that has a high probability of resulting in a developmental delay.** These diagnoses include conditions such as Down's syndrome and cerebral palsy, severe attachment disorders, and hearing and vision impairments secondary to exposure to toxic substances, such as alcohol.[14]

- **Children who have developmental delays as determined by state criteria** in one or more of the following areas of development: cognitive, physical, communication, social or emotional, and adaptive.[15]

States may elect to also provide IDEA Part C services to a third category:

- **Children "at risk" for developmental delays.** Ten states provide services to at-risk children under Part C.[16] These states use various factors to define "at-risk," some of which include: low birth weight, chronic lung disease, failure to thrive, parental substance abuse, poverty, parental developmental disability, parental age, parental education attainment, and child abuse and neglect.[17] A few other states have state law or regulations that provide for screening and tracking at-risk young children, but do not require Part C services for these children.[18]

Individualized family service plan: determining needs, services, and placement. Once a young child is found eligible under Part C, the next steps in the Part C process are similar to Part B of the IDEA: the Part C team must draft a written plan that first determines the needs, then

71

IDEA Part B Versus Part C: Distinguishing Factors

FACTOR	PART B	PART C
Ages Covered	Three—twenty one	Birth—three
Where to make referral for services	Local school or school district administrator, or State Department of Education.	Lead agency responsible for early intervention services; may be the State Department of Education but could also be Department of Health or other agency.
Eligibility requirements	Child must have one of the following disabilities: • speech/language impairments • autism • mental retardation • orthopedic impairments • emotional impairments • hearing impairments • traumatic brain injury • visual impairments • specific learning disability • other health impairments And in some states: • developmental delay	Child must: • be diagnosed with a mental or physical condition that has a high probability of resulting in developmental delay, or • have a state-defined developmental delay. Or, in some states, • be "at risk" for developmental delays
Service coordinator	Not applicable	Must be appointed to ensure coordination of needed services for the child and family
Evaluation	Only the child is evaluated	The child AND family are evaluated
Services	Geared primarily towards child, (as outlined in the IEP)	If needed, services provided to child AND family, (e.g., counseling, home visits)

FACTOR	PART B	PART C
IEP v. IFSP	IEP is formulated that describes child's disabilities, individualized services, goals and objectives, and appropriate placement.	IFSP is drafted that includes information about the child's delays, specific early intervention and appropriate setting.
Required attendees at IEP v. IFSP	Parent(s), regular education and special education teachers, qualified representative of the school with knowledge of curriculum and available resources, individual to interpret evaluation results (if not already present), the child when appropriate	Service coordinator, evaluator, parent(s)
Location of services	Usually school setting	Child's natural environment; can be home or center or school-based.
Parent refusal	School can request due process hearing to override parent's refusal	School cannot challenge parent's refusal of services
Review	Annual, but more often if requested	Every six months, and annually to evaluate and revise IFSP, but more often if requested

decides on services to be provided, and finally determines the appropriate setting for those services. For children under Part C this plan is called an individualized family service plan (IFSP). The IFSP must be in writing and include:

- present levels of child's development and functioning;
- statement of the family's resources, priorities and concerns;
- major expected outcomes;
- specific early interventions, including the frequency, intensity and method of delivery;
- the natural environments in which services will be provided;
- dates of services and their length;
- the service coordinator's name; and
- a plan for transitioning the child to preschool or other services.[19]

Services. Again, under Part C, the services are not just for the child, but the entire family. These can include:

- family training, counseling and home visits;
- special instruction;
- speech-language pathology and audiology services;
- health and nutrition services;
- occupational or physical therapy;
- psychological services;
- social work services;
- transportation to early intervention services;
- vision screenings; and
- assistive technology devices and services.[20]

Services can be provided to the foster family or the birth family, or both, depending on the case circumstances.

Location of Service Delivery. Part C of the IDEA states that services are to be delivered in the child's natural environment "to the maximum extent appropriate."[21] This may be a school, child care center, or the home. For children in foster care, determining the appropriate setting for services may be complicated by the involvement of the child's parents, foster parents, and caseworker. The natural setting for a child in care may depend on the permanency plan for the infant or toddler or on the ability for all involved with the young child to collaborate. For example, the appropriate setting may be in the home of the foster parent but may include the parent's participation. In other circumstances it may be appropriate to provide the services outside the home, perhaps in a child care facility or agency offices, where there is a better opportunity for professionals to observe interactions between the child and parents.

Parent Refusal. A parent or surrogate can refuse the services identified in the IFSP. There is no provision for the Part C entity to challenge a parent's refusal and ensure services are provided to the child. This refusal right under Part C makes the question of who makes education decisions for the child, already a critical issue under Part B of the IDEA, that much more important under Part C. Therefore, advocates need to pay close attention to who the legal education decision maker is for the young child and develop creative strategies for ensuring young children get the services they need. This may involve working closely with parents to ensure they understand and cooperate with the Part C process, or may involve judges taking a leadership role to ensure all parties are working together to meet the needs of the child.

Note: The following language appeared in the text of chapter 3, but the endnotes and citations are to Part C.

How Do I Determine Who Can Act as the Parent or if a Surrogate Parent Is Needed?

While usually an advocate can request a referral for evaluation of special education needs, only the parent or surrogate can consent to the evaluation or reevaluation of the child, and ultimately to the services put in place for the child. Therefore, when consents for evaluations need to be signed, it must be determined if a parent is available or if a surrogate needs to be appointed. The parent or the surrogate is the key decision maker for all IDEA-related issues, including services and placement, so clarity at the beginning of the process is critical.

The IDEA statute requires states to establish procedural safeguards to ensure children with disabilities receive a free and appropriate public education (FAPE). The law requires procedures to be in place when:
- the parents of the child are not known,
- the agency cannot, after reasonable efforts, locate the parents, or
- the child is a ward of the State.[1]

These procedures need to include the assignment of an individual as the surrogate when needed.[2]

To determine the need for a surrogate you must review the IDEA regulation; it defines parent as:
- **prong 1** "a natural or adoptive parent of the child;
- **prong 2** a guardian;
- **prong 3** a person acting in the place of a parent (such as a grandparent or stepparent with whom the child lives, or a person who is legally responsible for the child's welfare; or
- **prong 4** a surrogate parent…"[3]

Based on the four prongs of this definition, you can argue under the second and third prongs that guardians and relative caretakers or anyone with legal custody of a child (other than the state) have the same rights as a parent under IDEA. In some states foster parents are considered the parent under this third prong and do not need to be appointed as surrogates (see next section). It may be wise to get a court order to memorialize this legal arrangement.

Children in foster care without a person fitting the first three prongs of the definition of parent above, will need a surrogate parent. A surrogate parent sits in the shoes of the parents and makes decisions about special education services for the child. Federal law leaves the process of appointing a surrogate up to states. Consult state law, regulations, and policies to find out how your state appoints a surrogate when one is needed for a child in foster care.

Who Can be Appointed as a Surrogate for a Child in Foster Care?

Some states require anyone acting as the parent (people that fit under the third prong) to be officially appointed as a surrogate parent (under the forth prong), to make their role as the education decision maker even clearer. Be sure to consult your state law to determine the best way for these individuals to have the authority to be the child's decision maker. Federal law is clear that a surrogate parent cannot be an employee of any state agency, or a person or an employee of a person providing early intervention services to the child or family. [4] Therefore, child welfare agency personnel, including caseworkers, cannot be the surrogate parent for a child in foster care.

It is preferable that a surrogate be a person who knows about the child's needs. If the education decision maker cannot be the parent, guardian, or person acting in place of the parent, the next best option is to have a surrogate appointed who has some knowledge of the child. This may be the foster parent, a relative, a court appointed special advocate (CASA),[5] a child's attorney or guardian ad litem, or some other person involved in the child's life. The appropriateness of the individual will differ from state to state, and even from case to case. Preferably, the individual will understand the special education process, or at least be willing to learn and work with someone who can guide them through the process. For example, a relative may agree to be the surrogate, with assurances that the child's attorney will attend meetings and help advocate for the child. Specific procedures on who makes surrogate appointments may differ depending on state law, but often the school system is responsible for appointing surrogates.

A surrogate unknown to the child may be appointed for the child. Because at times the appointed surrogate may not know the child, and may not have any experience with the child welfare system or what it means for a child to be in foster care, this is the least desirable option. An advocate's role in this situation is to educate the surrogate on the foster care system, and the child's specific needs and situation.

How Can a Foster Parent be the Education Decision Maker?

The federal IDEA regulations clarify that foster parents may act as the parent, if:
• the "natural parent's authority to make decisions required of parents under the act has been extinguished under state law"; and

- the foster parent:
  - "has an ongoing, long-term parental relationship with the child,
  - is willing to make educational decisions under the act, and
  - has no interest that would conflict with the interests of the child."[6]

This regulation raises some questions:

Does "act as the parent" mean that an official surrogate appointment is unnecessary when a foster parent meets the above criteria? States vary on this issue; some have foster parents appointed as surrogates and others have foster parents act as the parent (prong 3) without a formal appointment. A strict reading of the language of the regulation certainly favors the latter.

What does "extinguished under state law" mean? Certainly a termination of parental rights (TPR) would end the parent's rights to make education decisions. Consult your state laws to determine if education decision-making rights of a parent of a child in foster care end before a TPR ruling. For example, Maryland allows by statute "limited guardianship" for education decisions to be given to the agency or an individual as early as the dispositional hearing when a parent is "unavailable, unwilling, or unable to consent to services that are in the best interest of the child."[7] If your state statute is unclear, a court may need to determine what factors to consider when deciding to strip a parent of education decision-making authority.

Another interpretation of the federal regulations could be that foster parents may "act as the parent" (prong 3) when decision-making authority has been extinguished (i.e., termination of parental rights), but before that time, foster parents may be appointed as surrogates.[8]

What would be "an interest that would conflict with the interests of the child?" Arguably, foster parents have some emotional and monetary interest in keeping a child in their care. What if foster parents, acting as surrogate parents, had to decide if a child was to be placed in a residential setting, meaning the child would be removed from her home? Would the foster parents' emotional bond with the child, or their need for foster care payments, affect their ability to make the best decisions for the child? Or, would a foster parent, who is perhaps burned out, agree to a residential placement for a child even though the child could be maintained in the community with appropriate services? Most foster parents do have the best interests of the child at heart and would not act in their own self-interest, but this does not change the issue of the appearance of, or the potential for, conflict.

If there is no clear individual in the child's life available to be appointed as the surrogate, a surrogate will be appointed for the child. Specific procedures, such as who appoints surrogates, may differ depending on state law, so be sure to consult your state statute or regulations. This is the least desirable option, because the appointed surrogate will not know the child, and may not have any experience with the child welfare system or what it means for a child to be in foster care. An advocate's role in this situation is to attempt to educate the surrogate on the foster care system, and the child's specific needs and situation.

Sources:

[1] 34 C.F.R § 303.406(a).

[2] 34 C.F.R. § 303.406(b) & (c).

[3] 34 C.F.R. § 303.19(a).

[4] 34 C.F.R. § 303.406(d).

[5] E.g., see Cal. Gov. Code § 7579.5: When appointing a surrogate parent, the local educational agency shall, as a first preference, select a relative caretaker, foster parent, or court-appointed special advocate, if any of these individuals exists and is willing and able to serve.

[6] 34 C.F.R. § 303.19(b).

[7] Annotated Code of Maryland, Courts and Judicial Proceedings §3-819(c)1(ii).

[8] E.g., see Nevada Department of Education. "The Appointment of Surrogate Parents for Students with Disabilities." February 2000.

Reviews. Part C requires the team to review the IFSP every six months in addition to an annual meeting to evaluate and revise the plan.[22] Since young children are developing and changing rapidly, frequent review of services and the child's needs are an important part of Part C.

Practice Tips:

- Make Part C referrals for children in foster care from birth to age three. Judges should include referrals in their court orders. Attorneys should advocate for referrals at hearings. Caseworkers and foster parents should raise the need for referral to all involved in the case.
- Help educate child welfare caseworkers of the requirement under CAPTA for procedures to be in place to make Part C referrals for children from birth to age three when there has been a substantiated abuse or neglect administrative finding.
- Review your state laws and regulations to determine how your state defines developmental delay and "at risk" of developmental delay if that category is used in your state.
- If cooperative, the parent should be involved in all aspects of the Part C process. Provide resources so the parent can make appropriate decisions for the child.
- If the parent is uncooperative or unable to participate, determine if someone else meets the definition of parent or if a surrogate is needed.

- Ensure the parent or surrogate attends all meetings related to Part C and actively participates in decisions regarding the child. Advocates can also attend the meetings by invitation by either the parent, surrogate, or the Part C entity.

Part B, Children Ages 3–5

Children over age three follow Part B of the IDEA (discussed in chapter 3) that applies to children with disabilities ages three to 21. Therefore, a child as young as three with a disability enumerated in IDEA (i.e., learning disability, emotional impairment, speech or language impairment) may qualify for an IEP and special education services.

In addition, Part B allows a special consideration for young children. For children ages three through nine, an additional category of "developmental delay" may be added to the categories of disabilities that qualify the child for services and an IEP in certain states and jurisdictions.[23] Both the state and the local education agency must agree to include "developmental delay" in the disability categories under Part B. This continuation of "developmental delay" for children over age three can benefit children in care. It can help avoid identifying a child with a disability too early, allowing for the possibility that the child will make gains by age nine and will no longer need special education services. The delay in identifying a child with a disability can ensure more accurate information about the child's needs is gathered as the child gets older, and help to more precisely identify the child's specific disability.

Another provision in IDEA allows families of children ages three through five to continue with an IFSP instead of requiring an IEP. In fact, three states use IFSPs for all preschool children, and 22 states allow local discretion in using IFSPs for preschoolers.[24] Children benefit from the family-centered supports provided with the IFSP but not required under an IEP. In addition, using the IFSP allows for continuity of services rather than forcing children into new programs and settings. A child in foster care can benefit from this continuity, as well as the additional family supports, regardless of whether those supports are for the parents, foster parents, relative caretakers, or preadoptive parents.

IDEA requires a transition plan in a child's IFSP to ensure a smooth transition from early intervention services to a preschool program.[25] This should include information to help the child adjust and function in the new setting. New evaluations must be completed so eligibility under Part B can be determined.

Practice Tips:

- If the child has been receiving Part C services, ensure smooth transitions from Part C to preschool services. This can include advocating for continued use of an IFSP if continued family services will benefit the child's development.
- If the child has not been receiving Part C services, begin the referral and evaluation process under Part B.
- Determine if the child's school system permits developmental delay as a category of disabilities under Part B.
- Help draft the child's IEP (or IFSP if applicable) and ensure appropriate services and placement are identified.
- Continue to monitor service delivery during these young, critical years, and ensure appropriateness of programs and services.

Part C Surrogate Parent Provisions
IDEA Statute: Part C—Infants and Toddlers with Disabilities
20 U.S.C. § 1439

(a) MINIMUM PROCEDURES The procedural safeguards required to be included in a statewide system under section 635(a)(13) shall provide, at a minimum, the following:

(5) Procedures to protect the rights of the infant or toddler whenever the parents of the infant or toddler are not known or cannot be found or the infant or toddler is a ward of the State, including the assignment of an individual (who shall not be an employee of the State lead agency, or other State agency, and who shall not be any person, or any employee of a person, providing early intervention services to the infant or toddler or any family member of the infant or toddler) to act as a surrogate for the parents.

IDEA Regulations:
34 C.F.R. § 303.19 Parent.

(a) General. As used in this part, "parent" means—
(1) A natural or adoptive parent of a child;
(2) A guardian;
(3) A person acting in the place of a parent (such as a grandparent or stepparent with whom the child lives, or a person who is legally responsible for the child's welfare); or
(4) A surrogate parent who has been assigned in accordance with Sec. 303.406.

(b) Foster parent. Unless State law prohibits a foster parent from acting as a parent, a State may allow a foster parent to act as a parent under Part C of the Act if—
(1) The natural parents' authority to make the decisions required of parents under the Act has been extinguished under State law; and

(2) The foster parent—
(i) Has an ongoing, long-term parental relationship with the child;
(ii) Is willing to make the decisions required of parents under the Act; and
(iii) Has no interest that would conflict with the interests of the child.

(Authority: 20 U.S.C. §1401(19), 1431-1445)

34 C.F.R. § 303.406 Surrogate parents.

(a) General. Each lead agency shall ensure that the rights of children eligible under this part are protected if—

    (1) No parent (as defined in Sec. 303.18) can be identified;

    (2) The public agency, after reasonable efforts, cannot discover the whereabouts of a parent; or

    (3) The child is a ward of the State under the laws of that State.

(b) Duty of lead agency and other public agencies. The duty of the lead agency, or other public agency under paragraph (a) of this section, includes the assignment of an individual to act as a surrogate for the parent. This must include a method for—

    (1) Determining whether a child needs a surrogate parent; and

    (2) Assigning a surrogate parent to the child.

(c) Criteria for selecting surrogates.

    (1) The lead agency or other public agency may select a surrogate parent in any way permitted under State law.

    (2) Public agencies shall ensure that a person selected as a surrogate parent—

        (i) Has no interest that conflicts with the interests of the child he or she represents; and

        (ii) Has knowledge and skills that ensure adequate representation of the child.

(d) Non-employee requirement; compensation.

    (1) A person assigned as a surrogate parent may not be—

        (i) An employee of any State agency; or

        (ii) A person or an employee of a person providing early intervention services to the child or to any family member of the child.

    (2) A person who otherwise qualifies to be a surrogate parent under paragraph (d)(1) of this section is not an employee solely because he or she is paid by a public agency to serve as a surrogate parent.

(e) Responsibilities. A surrogate parent may represent a child in all matters related to—

    (1) The evaluation and assessment of the child;

    (2) Development and implementation of the child's IFSPs, including annual evaluations and periodic reviews;

    (3) The ongoing provision of early intervention services to the child; and

    (4) Any other rights established under this part.

(Authority: 20 U.S.C. § 1439(a)(5))

CONCLUSION

Accessing services and quality programs for children from birth through age five will significantly affect the ability to achieve permanence for these young children. The education services and programs can also prevent re-entry into the child welfare system after a successful reunification, adoption, or other placement. Ultimately, education advocacy for young children can prevent later difficulties and lead to education success and brighter futures.

Endnotes

[1] Dicker, Sheryl & Elysa Gordon. "Early Intervention and Early Childhood Programs: Essential Tools for Child Welfare Advocacy." *Clearinghouse Review, Journal of Poverty Law and Policy* 34 (11-12), March-April 2001, 727.

[2] Se'ne'chal, M. & J. LeFevre. "Parental Involvement in the Development of Children's Reading Skill: A Five-Year Longitudinal Study." *Child Development* 73, 2002, 445-460.

[3] Snow, C.E., M.S. Burns, & P. Griffin, eds. "Preventing Reading Difficulties in Young Children." Washington, DC: National Academy Press, 1998.

[4] See, for example, Cicchetti, D., & S. Toth. "Child Maltreatment and Attachment Organization: Implications for Intervention." In *Attachment Theory: Social, Developmental, and Clinical Perspectives*. Edited by S. Goldberg, R. Muir, & J. Kerr. London: The Analytical Press, 1995, 279-308.

[5] Erickson, M. & B. Egeland. "Child Neglect." In *The APSAC Handbook on Child Maltreatment*. Edited by J. Briere et al.. Thousand Oaks, CA: Sage Publications, 1996, 4-20.

[6] See Silver, Judith A. "Starting Young." In *Young Children in Foster Care*. Baltimore: Paul H. Brookes, 1999, 12-13.

[7] See Silver, Judith A. "Emotional Development and Disorders in Young Children in the Child Welfare System." In *Young Children in Foster Care*. Baltimore: Paul H. Brookes, 1999, 47-53.

[8] Wulczyn, Fred & Kristen Hislop. "Babies in Foster Care: The Numbers Call for Attention." Washington, DC: Zero to Three, April-May 2002 <http://www.zerotothree.org/ztt_professionals.html>

[9] 42 U.S.C. § 1396d(e). See also http://www.nls.org/conf/epsdt.htm and http://www.healthlaw.org/index/shtml

[10] 42 U.S.C. § 1396d(r)(5).

[11] For more information, visit http://www.earlycare.org.

[12] 42 U.S.C. 5106a(b)(2)(A)(xxi) reads "provisions and procedures for referral of a child under the age of 3 who is involved in a substantiated case of child abuse or neglect to early intervention services funded under part C of the Individuals with Disabilities Education Act."

[13] 34 C.F.R. § 303.321(e).

[14] Dicker & Gordon, April 2001, 732.

[15] 34 C.F.R. § 303.16(a)(1) (2000).

[16] California, Guam, Hawaii, Indiana, Massachusetts, New Hampshire, Nevada, New Mexico, North Carolina and West Virginia. See Dicker, Sheryl & Elysa Gordon. "Early Intervention and Early Childhood Programs: Essential Tools for Child Welfare Advocacy." *Clearinghouse Review, Journal of Poverty Law and Policy* 34(11-12), March-April 2001, 732.

[17] Ibid.

[18] Two states that do so are New York (see McKinney's Public Health Law § 2542(1)(c)) and Pennsylvania (see 11 Pa. Cons. Stat. Ann. § 875-305)

[19] 20 U.S.C. § 1436(d).

[20] 20 U.S.C. § 1432(4)(E).

[21] 20 U.S.C. § 1432(4)(G).

[22] 34 C.F.R. § 303.342(b).

[23] 20 U.S.C. § 1401(3)(B).

[24] Maryland, Maine & Minnesota. Neas, Katherine Beh & Jennifer Mezey. "Addressing Child Care Challenges for Children with Disabilities: Proposals for CCDBG and IDEA Reauthorizations." Washington, DC: Center for Law and Social Policy, February 24, 2003, 8. <http://www.clasp.org/DMS/Documents/1046108337.25/clasp_ES.pdf>.

[25] 20 U.S.C. § 1436(d).

What the Science Shows

Developmental effects of child maltreatment

Research over the last four decades reveals that children who are maltreated often experience disrupted growth and development. Maltreatment can hinder healthy physical, cognitive, emotional, and social development in later childhood and adulthood.[1] These developmental delays add a challenging hurdle to an already difficult task of meeting the education needs of young children in foster care.

Socioemotional disorders & cognitive delays. A 1987 longitudinal study included a proportion of children whose mothers were neglectful and/or emotionally unavailable; some were also exposed to physical abuse. Follow-up findings showed these children to be socially withdrawn, inattentive, and cognitively underachieving in their elementary-school years.[2]

Fetal alcohol spectrum disorders (FASD). Children in foster care who were exposed prenatally to alcohol may develop FASDs—a range of birth defects that can cause developmental delays, risk of speech-language problems, attention deficits, impulsive and hyperactive behavior, growth problems, cardiac abnormalities and mental retardation.[3]

Separation & attachment disorders. Young children in foster care are often negatively affected by separation from their parents and placement with a new, often unfamiliar, caregiver. These children can experience grief and rage as a result of the removal from their home and often limited visitation with their parents.[4] Entry into foster care may also lead to multiple placements and caretakers, causing further trauma and attachment difficulties. Mental health problems may also result, such as post traumatic stress disorder, regulatory disorders, attachment disorders, depressive disorders, and anxiety disorders.[5]

Early interventions that make a difference

Permanent placements. A 1998 study involved 25 children from 2 to 4 years, who were being raised in a Romanian orphanage and seriously delayed in their cognitive and social functioning. The age these children entered adoptive homes was shown to predict improved cognitive development of these children by age four. Specifically, being adopted before the age of six months predicted later healthy development.[6]

Quality care and education settings. In addition to permanent placements, high quality care and education settings also can have a positive impact on young children. Research shows that participating in quality early care:

* helps children prepare for school;
* improves early scores on standardized tests;
* reduces the need for special education services or the need to repeat grades in school; and
* improves graduation rates, college attendance, and employment outcomes.[7]

Targeted early intervention services. Of the young children in foster care, over half experience some developmental delays. This is four-to-five times the rate among children not in foster care.[8] However, in a 1995 study of children in foster care under three years who lived in three urban areas, only 10% were receiving services for developmental delays.[9] Research shows that intensive, early intervention services can help reduce the harm young children in foster care face through their exposure to the many risk factors discussed above.[10]

Focusing on quality early education and intervention services can also help prevent child abuse and neglect. This is especially true among children in care with special needs. Research shows that children with developmental delays and disabilities are at higher risk to be maltreated.[11] However, according to a recent national study of the Early Head Start Program, three-year-old children participating in Early Head Start were overall less likely to be spanked or to be hospitalized due to injuries or accidents, and parents of these children showed positive changes in parenting knowledge.[12]

Sources:

[1]See, for example, Cicchetti , D. & S. Toth. "Child Maltreatment and Attachment Organization: Implications for Intervention." In *Attachment Theory: Social, Developmental, and Clinical Perspectives.* Edited by S. Goldberg, R. Muir, & J. Kerr. London: The Analytical Press, 1995, 279-308.

[2]Erickson, M. & B. Egeland. "Child Neglect." In *The APSAC Handbook on Child Maltreatment,* edited by J. Briere et al. Thousand Oaks, CA: Sage Publications, 1996, 4-20.

[3]See Silver, Judith A. "Starting Young." In *Young Children in Foster Care.* Baltimore: Paul H. Brookes, 1999, 12-13.

[4]See Silver, Judith A. "Emotional Development and Disorders in Young Children in the Child Welfare System." In *Young Children in Foster Care.* Baltimore: Paul H. Brookes, 1999, 38.

[5]Ibid., 47-53.

[6]Rutter, M. & the English and Romanian Adoptees (ERA) Study Team. "Developmental Catchup and Deficit, Following Adoption After Severe Global Early Deprivation." *Journal of Child Psychology and Psychiatry* 39, 1998, 465-476.

[7]See http://www.earlycare.org/factsheet1.htm.

[8]Dicker, Sheryl. "Improving the Odds for the Healthy Development of Young Children in Foster Care." In *Promoting the Emotional Well Being of Children and Families National Center for Children in Poverty Policy Paper #2,* 2001, 3.

[9]Dicker, Sheryl & Elysa Gordon. "Early Intervention and Early Childhood Programs: Essential Tools for Child Welfare Advocacy." *Clearinghouse Review, Journal of Poverty Law and Policy* 34 (11-12), March-April 2001, 727.

[10]Dicker, 2001, 6.

[11]See Silver, Judith A. "Child Abuse and Developmental Disabilities." In *Young Children in Foster Care.* Baltimore: Paul H. Brookes, 1999.

[12]See *Making a Difference in the Lives of Infants and Toddlers and Their Families: The Impacts of Early Head Start. Vol. 1: Final Technical Report.* Washington, DC: U.S. Department of Health and Human Services, June 2001.

Developmental Checklist for Young Children

This resource on child development can be given to the child's caregivers and caseworkers to improve understanding of healthy development and to look for signs of problems.

This checklist is designed for you to record your child's growth and development. There is space to fill in the age when your child begins each activity.

When you fill in the checklist, remember that each child develops at his or her own pace. The age listed on the checklist is the time a number of children are consistently doing the activity.

If your child is not doing one activity at the age listed, there is probably no need to be concerned. However, if your child is late in doing several activities, you should discuss it with your child's doctor.

If your child was born prematurely, ask the doctor about your child's corrected developmental age.

Usual Activities During...

Birth to 3 Months
____Able to raise head from surface when lying on tummy
____Makes eye contact with adults
____Moves arms and legs in energetic manner
____Smiles and coos
____Grunts and sighs
____Likes to be held and rocked

3 to 5 Months
____Eyes follow a slow-moving object
____Able to hold head erect
____Grasps objects when placed in his or her hand
____Laughs out loud
____Anticipates feeding and recognizes familiar faces
____Sits briefly with support

5 to 7 Months
____Reaches for, holds and bangs objects
____Stretches out arm to be picked up
____Babbles
____Runs towards sounds
____Holds cookie or cracker-begins chewing
____Rolls over

7 to 9 Months

___Can sit steadily for about five minutes

___Can transfer object from one hand to the other

___Creeps (pulling body with arms and leg kicks)

___Responds to name

___Can stand for short time holding on to support

___Likes to play peek-a-boo

9 to 12 Months

___Says "Ma-ma" or "Da-da"

___Copies sounds

___Waves "hi" or "bye"

___Able to pull self up at side of crib or playpen

___Walks holding on to furniture

___Takes sips from a cup

___Crawls on hands and knees

___Hits two objects together; throws and drops objects

12 to 15 Months

___Says several words besides "Ma-ma/Da-da"

___Walks without support by 15 months

___Finger feeds self

___Explores toys

15 to 18 Months

___Uses 10 to 15 words spontaneously

___Scribbles on paper after shown how

___Begins using a spoon

___Drinks from cup held in both hands

___Cooperates with dressing

___Walks across a large room

18 to 24 Months

___Can build a tower with three blocks

___Likes to climb and take things apart

___Uses single words frequently

___Begins two-word phrases

___Able to run

___Looks at pictures in a book

Sidebar 6 continued

2 to 3 Years

___Walks up/down stairs using alternate feet, while holding on

___Says at least 100 words

___Uses three-word phrases

___Points to objects in a book

___Knows his or her sex, body parts

___Jumps lifting both feet off ground

3 to 4 Years

___Opens a door by turning the door knob

___Builds a tower with nine blocks

___Follows commands of on, under or behind (e.g., "stand on the rug.")

___Names pictures in a book or magazine

___Understands complex sentences

___Uses action words

4 to 5 Years

___Uses four- to five-word sentences

___Stands on one foot

___Throws a ball overhand

___Enjoys active play: racing, hopping, climbing

___Points while counting three different objects

___Names three colors

___Counts aloud 1 through 10

___Can copy a cross

5 to 6 Years

___Can copy a square

___Asks questions to seek information

___Tells age correctly

___Skips with both feet

___Catches a small ball on a bounce

___Dresses him/herself completely

SCHOOL DISCIPLINE

INTRODUCTION

A recent study in a midwest community of 262 older youth in foster care revealed 73% had been suspended at least once since the seventh grade and 16% had been expelled.[1] Keeping schools safe and free from distractions from learning has become difficult as school violence increases across the country. Punitive actions for students who violate school rules are common ways to control classrooms and student behavior. Many punishments exist, from suspension and expulsion to written referrals or in-school detentions, or even corporal punishment (see sidebar #1).

This chapter looks at school discipline, how it impacts children in foster care, and what advocates can do to:

- prevent disciplinary actions from being necessary;
- ensure appropriate disciplinary procedures are followed and punishments are fair; and
- minimize disruption to the child's educational progress and future academic success.

WHAT IS SCHOOL DISCIPLINE?

School systems typically develop student codes of conduct, and make the information available to all students. The codes outline acceptable and unacceptable school behaviors. They usually inform students of the possible consequences of failing to comply with school rules. Consequences include:

- **Written referrals.** Child receives written notice of a disciplinary code violation and a note goes in the student's record. It is often used to document minor and first offenses.
- **Detentions.** Child is removed from class for a period during the school day or required to spend time in a punishment room after school.
- **Short-term suspensions.** Child is not permitted to attend school, or school-related activities for a period, typically under 10 days.
- **Long-term suspensions.** Child is not permitted to attend school or school-related activities for a period over 10 days. These suspensions can last until the end of a semester or the end of a school year.
- **Expulsions.** Child is not permitted to return to school indefinitely. While this could mean forever, most schools have procedures for a child to petition for return to school after a period, such as the beginning of the next school year. For example, if a student has been expelled for bringing marijuana to school, and during the expulsion period has enrolled in a drug treatment program, the student may be able to petition the school for readmission after the initial expulsion has passed. The agreement to allow the student back may involve conditions, such as attending a special school or program for students in

substance abuse recovery. When a student has been expelled from one school system, re-enrollment in another school system is sometimes possible. However, neighboring school systems will often honor the other school system's disciplinary measure and not permit enrollment until after the period of suspension or expulsion imposed by the other jurisdiction. While some school systems may provide some kind of education program for expelled children, often these youth receive no education during the expulsion period.

HOW DISCIPLINE AFFECTS CHILDREN IN FOSTER CARE

Discipline impacts all students, but is particularly damaging for children in foster care. Some consequences include:

Stigma

Children in foster care may already feel stigmatized by their involvement in the child welfare system and the courts. The "troublemaker" or "bad" student label can further compound that stigma, and add to the ways they feel different from their peers.

Emotional Impact

Many of these children already suffer from low self-esteem and self-worth. Discipline in the school system may exacerbate these issues.

Academic Impact

Besides the emotional impact, there can be a profound academic impact to disciplinary action. Detentions, suspensions, and expulsions often cause children to miss important class time and assignments.

Sidebar 1

Corporal Punishment in Schools

While corporal punishment in school is not as common as it once was, it is still permitted in many states.[1] According to the National Center to Abolish Corporal Punishment in Schools (NCACPS), 21 states still permit schools to use corporal punishment on students. While many school systems in those states have policies against such punishment, corporal punishment is taking place in many schools across the country. The NCACPS reports 342,038 incidents of reported corporal punishment in schools in the 1999-2000 school year.

Practice Tips :

• Find out if the school a child is attending permits corporal punishment.

• Consider whether to alert the school to the child's abuse and neglect history. Talk to the child about their feelings about having this information shared.

• If you decide to share the child's history, alert the appropriate school official, principal, or teacher, preferably the individual who is responsible for administering corporal punishment of students.

• Meet with the school official and explain the effect that such methods may have on the child and possible emotional harm that such measures may cause.

• Discuss the possibility of an agreement to use other disciplinary measures for the child. If no such agreement can be reached, ensure the child's file is documented to reflect the added concerns about this method of punishment. The goal is to ensure that if the child is subjected to corporal punishment at school, the school will consider the child's abuse and neglect history.

Sources:
[1] See http://www.stophitting.org/disatschool/statesBanning.php

Children in foster care may already have missed school days and be behind in their classwork. This could be caused by:

• the removal from their home and placement in foster care leading to a school change and a delay in re-enrollment;

• the need to attend court hearings, counseling, or medical appointments related to the abuse and neglect; or

• a lengthy period of distraction or inability to focus on school based on troubles at home, which may predate child welfare and court system intervention.

A long-term suspension or expulsion may lead a youth in foster care, already behind and at risk for dropping out of school, to decide to leave school without graduating.

Impact on Permanency

When children are in foster care, the goal is to find a permanent placement for them as quickly as possible. If the child is known to have behavior difficulties, permanent placement becomes more challenging. Trouble at school resulting in suspension or expulsion can disrupt a plan for permanent placement. Without the daily structure provided by attending school, many children in foster care become involved in delinquent or criminal activity. For example, a long-term suspension or an expulsion from school may cause working foster parents (who may have been considering adoption), to have the child removed from the home, due to the foster parents' inability to appropriately supervise the child during the day. Such a disciplinary action could also jeopardize a reunification effort when a parent, just getting back on her feet, is similarly unable to supervise a child who has been put out of school. Finally, it may be difficult to find a new permanent placement for a youth who is out of school with possible delinquent or criminal charges pending.

ADVOCACY ROLE

At times the "foster care" label or lack of a strong advocate may cause unnecessary or increased disciplinary issues for children in foster care. One or more strong advocates can step forward for a child and (1) help prevent disciplinary measures from being necessary, (2) protect the child's rights during disciplinary meetings and hearings, and (3) help minimize the effects of disciplinary actions.

(1) Prevent Discipline

Advocates can take steps to minimize the possibility of school discipline for a child in care. The first step is to understand why children in foster care may act out in school. For example, a child in foster care who has been severely beaten may react aggressively when adults have physical contact with him.

As a preventative measure, if a child is known to have challenging behaviors, or known to react negatively in certain situations, an advocate can take the following steps before a disciplinary incident:

- Ask for a school meeting to discuss possible interventions that will help the child's behavior improve.
- Explore techniques the school can use to interact with the child and address particular behaviors.
- Explore less punitive methods of discipline, such as positive reinforcement and behavior modification models. These models focus on changing the environment that is causing the behavior as opposed to changing the individual. For youth in foster care with behaviors that are linked to their experiences (e.g., child who had been locked in a closet becomes irate if placed in a timeout room), changing the environment may be the more appropriate approach.
- Collaborate with other child welfare system advocates and the child. When the child's attorney or GAL, caseworker, parent, foster parent, and therapist, among others, come together with the child to brainstorm about ways to address challenging behaviors, a unified approach can result. This can help show the child that many people care, and also give the child guidance on where to turn if they have a problem in school. Also, when child welfare system professionals present themselves as a unified front, communicating with the school system may become easier.

These methods can keep children safe and schools free from disruptions, but strong advocacy is needed to ensure constructive techniques are being used. Note that if a child is eligible for special

Sidebar 2

ABA Policy: School Discipline "Zero Tolerance" Policies, February 2001

RESOLVED, that the American Bar Association supports the following principles concerning school discipline:

- schools should have strong policies against gun possession and be safe places for students to learn and develop;

- in cases involving alleged student misbehavior, school officials should exercise sound discretion that is consistent with principles of due process and considers the individual student and the particular circumstances of misconduct; and

- alternatives to expulsion or referral for prosecution should be developed that will improve student behavior and school climate without making schools dangerous; and

FURTHER RESOLVED, that the ABA opposes, in principle, "zero tolerance" policies that have a discriminatory effect, or mandate either expulsion or referral of students to juvenile or criminal court, without regard to the circumstances or nature of the offense or the student's history.

education services (see section below), a preventative measure against disciplinary issues can include making accommodations in the child's individualized education program (IEP) (see sidebar #3), conducting a functional behavioral assessment (FBA), and drafting a behavioral intervention plan (BIP) (see further discussion below).

(2) Ensure Procedural Protections Are in Place

When disciplinary measures are taken against children in foster care, it is important to understand the procedural protections in place for all students who are disciplined. These protections are the same for youth in foster care as they are for non-foster youth, but do differ depending on whether the child is in a general education program or receiving special education services. (See chapter 2 for

information on legal developments shaping these procedural protections.)

General education discipline

Public school systems have great discretion when creating and implementing disciplinary rules and regulations.[2] Zero tolerance policies that mandate punishments for offenses, without considering the facts surrounding an incident, have increased over the past decade. A 2001 American Bar Association resolution opposes zero tolerance policies that mandate expulsion or referral to the court system without considering the circumstances or nature of the offense, or the student's history.[3]

Additionally, there are minimum due process protections that schools must afford students accused of school violations. These protections vary based on the type of discipline imposed.

Examples of Behavior Accommodations or Modifications That Can be Used in a Child's IEP

Note: These are examples of the type of accommodations that can be considered for a child. When drafting an IEP or §504 plan, make sure accommodations are tailored to the needs of each child.

- Arrange a "check-in" time to organize the day.

- Pair the student with a student who is a good behavior model for class projects.

- Modify school rules that may discriminate against the student.

- Use nonverbal cues to remind the student of rule violations.

- Amend consequences for rule violations (e.g., reward a forgetful student for remembering to bring pencils to class, rather than punishing the failure to remember).

- Minimize punishment. Provide positive as well as negative consequences.

- Develop an individualized behavioral intervention plan that is positive and consistent with the student's abilities and skills.

- Increase the frequency and immediacy of reinforcement.

- Arrange for the student to leave the classroom voluntarily and go to a designated "safe place" when under high stress.

- Develop a system or a code word to let the student know when behavior is not appropriate.

- Ignore behaviors that are not seriously disruptive.

- Develop interventions for behaviors that are annoying but not deliberate (e.g., provide a small piece of foam rubber for the desk of a student who continually taps a pencil on the desktop).

- Be aware of behavior changes that relate to medication or the length of the school day; modify expectations if appropriate.

Excerpt from School Accommodations and Modifications, from Families and Advocates Partnership for Education (FAPE), PACER Center Inc.

Suspensions under 10 days. Case law establishes minimum protections for students suspended for under 10 days.[4] These minimum protections are:

- Notice of violation
- Opportunity to refute charges
- Explanation of evidence relied upon

Schools may have additional procedures for these short-term suspensions, including some limited appeal process to a higher level administrator within the system. Some school districts also may have provisions for providing instruction through alternate means (e.g., sending work home, placing the student in a "suspension" class or site) during short-term suspensions.

Suspensions and expulsions over 10 days. When students are suspended for over 10 days or expelled, case law suggests some additional due process protections than those listed above may be warranted.[5] However, schools are free to determine what those due process protections look like. In most schools, students at risk of long-term suspension or expulsion have a right to an administrative hearing, where they can call witnesses and present their case before a neutral hearing officer. Often there are procedures for appealing the case before the school board and ultimately a court.

Practice Tips:

- Know your state and district school discipline policy. Search state and local school web sites. Keep a copy of the policies for each school district children may attend.
- If your district has a zero tolerance policy, examine the policy to determine if the school has any discretion over

whether to follow through with a sanction. If there is discretion, argue the facts of the case and present the child's circumstances at the disciplinary hearing.

- Involve a legal advocate for the child when available. An attorney may be best suited to present a case for the child at a disciplinary hearing, as the hearing process is similar to a court proceeding. A legal advocate may be necessary if the case needs to be appealed to court. The legal advocate could be the child's attorney, the agency attorney or the parent's attorney, depending on the facts of the case.

- Obtain supporting documentation from others involved in the child's life that may be persuasive to the hearing officer (e.g., coach, teacher, therapist, caseworker, foster parent).

- Ensure the child understands the process and understands what rule he or she is accused of violating (e.g., Did the child recently transfer into this school, and is the discipline policy different from his last school? Was the student ever provided a copy of the new disciplinary code?).

- Pursue appeals when warranted. While there are limited appeal avenues for suspensions under 10 days, appeals are usually options to challenge long-term suspensions and expulsions and may be warranted.

- If the child was also arrested for the act that led to the suspension, be aware of the interplay between the suspension hearing process and the court process. Coordinate your activities with the child's attorney in the delinquency or criminal matter.

Discipline for students with disabilities

When children receiving special education services under the Individuals with Disabilities Education Act (IDEA) are the subject of disciplinary sanctions, special procedural protections apply. The protections were developed out of concern that children with disabilities were being disciplined at a higher rate than their nondisabled peers. As a result, these protections refocus school IEP teams on the services the child is receiving (and accommodations being made related to problem behaviors) instead of on punitive measures that will remove the child from the classroom. These disciplinary protections also apply to children eligible under Section 504. (See sidebar 4 for further information.)(Note: the remainder of this section refers to eligibility under IDEA only; however these provisions equally apply to Section 504.)

Suspensions under 10 days

What constitutes a removal? Many of the protections under IDEA begin when a child has been removed for more than 10 days. It is therefore important to determine what constitutes a removal. While much of this determination will be interpretation, advocates need to think about whether a child was provided access to their education. While the law and regulations are clear that a suspension from school constitutes a day of removal, what about a child sent to the principal's office for most of the school day? Or a child placed in a timeout room? Or a child whose foster parent was called and asked to pick the child up from school, but the child was not under a formal disciplinary action? Advocates must be ready to argue that these situations may be a removal.

Functional Behavioral Assessments (FBA) and Behavioral Intervention Plans (BIP). An FBA is an assessment to determine a child's problem behaviors, to help determine what circumstances (i.e., environmental factors and surrounding events) result in the challenging behaviors. A BIP includes helpful interventions the school should use to address the problem behaviors with a goal of eliminating or decreasing them. For example:

Tania has been exhibiting negative behaviors at school. Her special education teacher has observed that these negative behaviors tend to occur on Wednesday mornings. The teacher contacts Tania's foster mother who reveals that Tania has been visiting with her mother on Tuesday evenings each week. At these visits, Tania is inundated with promises from her mother about returning to her care, even though her mother has repeatedly failed to complete her drug treatment program. Through this communication between the school and the foster mother, it becomes apparent that there may be a connection between Tania's frustration with her mother after her weekly visits and her outbursts the following morning. The teacher has an FBA completed and the team drafts a BIP that allows Tania to leave class on Wednesday morning to spend time with a trusted teacher.

FBAs are typically completed by a child's teacher and parent; for children in foster care, that can include a foster parent, caregiver, or other school and child welfare personnel who are familiar with the child's behaviors. An IEP team will then meet to review an FBA and draft a BIP.

Sidebar 4

Section 504 and Discipline

The special Individuals with Disabilities Education Act (IDEA) discipline procedures also apply to students with disabilities covered under Section 504 of the Rehabilitation Act. This includes the right to a manifestation hearing and determination for cases involving over 10 days of suspension or expulsion. However, should a student with a 504 plan be determined to not have a nexus between the disability and the misconduct, the student with a 504 plan can be suspended or expelled. There is also no requirement that the student continue to receive a free and appropriate public education as there is for students with individualized education programs (IEPs).

The best use of FBAs and BIPs is to prevent the need for discipline. By developing interventions to address all of the child's inappropriate behaviors, the IEP team prevents misconduct. Developing these plans before misconduct occurs, or after short-term suspensions, is recommended. However, often a disciplinary action occurs for a child with an IEP who does not have a BIP, or a child who has a BIP but the plan did not account for this particular misconduct. IDEA requires that within 10 days of commencing a disciplinary action of over 10 days, the IEP team must meet to conduct an FBA and develop a BIP if the student does not already have one in place or review and revise an existing plan.[6]

Suspensions and expulsions over 10 days

Manifestation hearing. For children receiving special education services, or suspected of having a disability, and at risk of a disciplinary action of over 10 days, the IDEA requires the school to hold a manifestation hearing, and to provide services that will enable the student to "appropri-

ately progress in the general curriculum and advance toward achieving the goals set out in the child's IEP."[7] Not only does this apply to a suspension or expulsion of 10 consecutive days or more, but potentially to shorter suspensions that total 10 days during the school year. Multiple short-term suspensions can be considered over 10 days if the different incidents constitute a pattern of removal.[8] The district's disciplinary policy will often specify whether removal of a student for part of a school day (e.g., teacher removals) is counted as a full day of suspension. The IEP team must convene the manifestation hearing "immediately, if possible, but in no case later than" the tenth day to review the disciplinary decision.[9] At the manifestation hearing, the following must be considered:

- **IEP appropriateness and implementation.** If an IEP already existed, the team must decide whether the IEP was appropriate for the child's needs and whether it was being implemented. If the IEP was not appropriate or was not being implemented appropriately, the child must return to school and the team must

97

immediately address the limitations of the child's IEP. For example:

David's IEP provides that an aide accompany him between classes. On a day the aide is absent from school, David pulls the fire alarm while unsupervised between second and third period and causes the evacuation of the entire school. Because David's IEP provided a solution to this misbehavior, and the reason for the misbehavior was the IEP was not being followed, David should not be disciplined for the misconduct.

- **Relationship between disability and behavior.** If the IEP was being administered appropriately, the team must next review the relation between the behavior that led to the discipline and the child's disability. If the team finds a nexus between the child's action and the disability, the child must return to school and the child's IEP (and BIP) should be revised to keep such an action from reoccurring. For example:

If Betty, a student with ADHD and impulsivity issues, throws an orange at a teacher because she became frustrated during class. The team finds that there was a nexus between her impulsive action and her ADHD diagnosis.

If the team decides that there was no nexus between the action and the disability, the child may be subject to the same disciplinary proceedings that would apply to a regular education student. However, remember that an IDEA-eligible student must have their IEP implemented, even if subjected to long-term suspension or expulsion (see section below).

- **If no IEP, should there have been?** Sometimes someone close to the child suspects the child has unaddressed special education needs. Even if the child has not been identified as needing special education services, requesting a manifestation hearing may be appropriate if the school knew, or should have known, that the child had a disability.[10] All of the manifestation hearing provisions discussed in this section will apply to children in this situation. If the school did not know the child had a disability before the violation, the school may pursue regular disciplinary proceedings. However, if an evaluation of the child is requested while the disciplinary matter is pending, the evaluation must be expedited.[11] A school may choose to delay the disciplinary matter until the expedited evaluation is completed.

- **Interim Alternative Educational Setting (IAES).** Even for cases involving drugs or weapons, a school must return the child to school after a manifestation hearing determines there was a nexus between the misconduct and the disability. The school may, however, place the child in an IAES for up to 45 days.[12] Also, if an administrative hearing officer determines that a child presents a safety risk to himself or others, the child may be placed in an IAES for up to 45 days.[13]

The IAES must be a setting that can implement the child's IEP. Therefore, the setting must be able to provide all of the related services and meet the goals and objectives outlined in the child's

IEP. This can be a special school, or a separate classroom within a school. Advocates should be concerned if the IAES a school is using consists of home tutoring for a few hours each week. The question advocates should ask is "Can a few hours of home tutoring implement everything in the child's IEP?"

- **IDEA-eligible students must have their IEPs implemented.** Even if a manifestation hearing team decides the child's behavior was not related to a disability, and the school proceeds with the disciplinary action (i.e., long-term suspension or expulsion), under IDEA, the child still must have an IEP implemented.[14] While a school may have some discretion as to where the child will be educated, the setting must allow the IEP to be implemented. (See sidebar #4 for a critical distinction between this rule and children with disabilities under Section 504 of the Rehabilitation Act.)

- Advocate for and review FBAs and BIPs when appropriate, and determine if they are addressing the appropriate behavioral issues. Advocate for the creation of a plan before a discipline problem develops.
- Ensure a child with an IEP or §504 is not put out of school more than 10 cumulative days without the school holding a manifestation meeting.
- Ensure a manifestation meeting is scheduled. If the school does not schedule this required meeting on its own, request a manifestation meeting in writing.
- Ensure the parent, person acting as the parent or the surrogate parent has

gotten notice of the meeting and is able to attend the meeting. (See chapter 3 for a full discussion of education decision-making authority).

- Attend and advocate for the child at manifestation hearings and other meetings and hearings related to discipline. Even if you are not the legal decision maker, you can provide information to the team that may affect the ultimate team decision.
- Ensure these questions are being addressed at the manifestation meeting: Was there an appropriate IEP? Was the IEP being implemented? Was there a nexus between the behavior and the disability? It is often important to involve the child's caseworker, therapist, medical providers, or other advocates at this hearing. These individuals may be able to provide the team with more information about the manner in which the child's disability presents itself.
- Request a manifestation hearing for a child who lacks an IEP if you think the school knew, or should have known the child had a disability that was having an educational impact. (See chapter 3 for a discussion of disabilities under IDEA.)
- If the child is placed in an interim alternative education setting (IAES), ensure the child's IEP is still being implemented.
- If you disagree with the team decision following a manifestation hearing, or with decisions made regarding the placement of a child in an IAES, the IDEA permits the parent or surrogate to appeal through an expedited due process hearing (see chapter 3 for more on due process hearings).

- Ensure students with IEPs who are suspended or expelled still receive a free appropriate public education.

(3) Minimize How Discipline Affects Foster Youth

Even when discipline is warranted, have the circumstances around the child's foster care involvement been considered when issuing the sanction? Are there other sanctions that could be used that would not negatively affect the child's education?

When considering sharing information about the child's abuse and neglect history or child welfare system involvement, think about confidentiality. Many youth do not want this information shared with school personnel. Their concerns may be based on a desire to keep this sensitive information private, or a fear of unfair treatment by school personnel who lack adequate training to understand what involvement with the child welfare system means. Even for advocates who must decide what is in the child's best interest (and do not advocate expressly for their desires), the child's position on this issue must be strongly considered.

Practice Tips:

- Ensure child's involvement in the foster care system is considered when appropriate. Does the decision maker for the disciplinary measure understand the child's situation and how child welfare involvement may have contributed to misbehavior or misconduct?
- Consider how the child feels about sharing details of foster care involvement with the school. Would sharing the private information about the child cause the child to be unfairly treated?

- The school district's disciplinary code may prescribe a range of possible consequences for acts that are subject to disciplinary action. Suggest alternatives to discipline that will not interfere with the child's educational progress (e.g., afterschool volunteer work, weekend community projects).

Discipline that leads to juvenile justice involvement

More frequently, schools are referring disciplinary cases to the juvenile justice system and law enforcement authorities. In many states, schools may initiate and file delinquency petitions (as well as unruly, and status offense petitions) in court that are related to school behaviors.[15] Advocates need to pay attention to what types of actions are resulting in these petitions. Recent reports show an increase in minor misconduct in schools resulting in court petitions and juvenile justice involvement.[16]

While IDEA does not prohibit the school from reporting criminal acts by children with disabilities to appropriate law enforcement authorities, advocates need to watch these cases closely. The law does require the school to provide special education and disciplinary records to the authorities when they report the crime.[17] However, advocates need to consider whether children with disabilities are being criminalized for behaviors that school systems are required under IDEA to address in the children's IEPs.[18] Strong special education advocacy is needed to ensure that schools are providing the appropriate services to children, and that the failure to provide these services does not result in juvenile or adult detention.

- Know education law, particularly IDEA.
- Ensure delinquency petitions are not being adjudicated for issues that should be addressed in a school setting and through appropriate school programming for the child.
- Ensure that appropriate special education and disciplinary records accompany reports to law enforcement about a child with special education needs.

CONCLUSION

Advocacy is needed to prevent and minimize the effects of discipline for children in foster care. Severe discipline, such as long-term suspension or expulsion, can compromise academic success for children in care, which ultimately affects their chances of achieving permanency and their futures. By understanding the disciplinary policies and processes in school systems, advocates can help ensure that children in foster care are disciplined fairly.

Endnotes

[1] McMillen, Curtis, et al. "Educational Experiences and Aspirations of Older Youth in Foster Care." *Child Welfare* 82, July/August 2003, 475.

[2] See Wood v. Strickland, 420 U.S. 308 (1975).

[3] For the full text of the resolution, see sidebar #2.

[4] See Goss v. Lopez, 419 U.S. 565 (1975).

[5] Ibid., 584. ("Longer suspensions or expulsions for the remainder of the school term, or permanently, may require more formal procedures."). For further discussion, see Brady, Kevin. "Weapon of Choice: Zero Tolerance School Discipline Policies and the Limitations of Student Procedural Due Process." *Children's Legal Rights Journal* 22(1), Spring 2002, 2.

[6] 20 U.S.C. § 1415 (k)(B)(i)-(ii).

[7] 34 C.F.R. § 300.121(d)(2).

[8] 20 U.S.C. § 1415 (k): A "series of removals constitute a pattern because they cumulate to more than 10 school days in a school year, and because of factors such as the length of each removal, the total amount of time the child is removed, and the proximity of the removals to one another."

[9] 20 U.S.C. §1415(k)(4).

[10] 20 U.S.C. §1415 (k)(8)(B). The school will be deemed to have knowledge if the parent of the child has expressed concern in writing, the behavior or performance of the child demonstrates the need for such services, the parent had requested an evaluation of the child, or the teacher of the child had expressed concern about the behavior of the child to appropriate school officials.

[11] 20 U.S.C. § 1415 (k)(8)(C).

[12] 20 U.S.C. §1415 (k)(1)(A)(ii).

[13] 20 U.S.C. §1415 (k)(2).

[14] See both 20 U.S.C. § 1415 (k)(5) and 1412 (a)(1) (a free and appropriate public education is available to all children with disabilities...including children with disabilities who have been suspended or expelled from school).

[15] Ordover, Eileen L. *When Schools Criminalize Disability/Education Law Strategies for Legal Advocates.* Washington, DC: Center for Law and Education, 2002, Introduction n.3. <http://cleweb.org/Downloads/when_schools_criminalize_disabil.htm>.

[16] See Rimer, Sara. "Unruly Students Facing Arrest, Not Detention." *The New York Times*, January 4, 2004.

[17] 20 U.S.C. § 1415 (k)(9).

[18] For an in-depth discussion of this issue, see Ordover, 2002.

CREATIVE WAYS TO MEET EDUCATION NEEDS

INTRODUCTION

How do you help children in foster care succeed in school? You don't have to start from scratch. This chapter considers four ways to meet education needs for children in foster care:

- direct advocacy
- courtroom attention
- legislation
- interagency collaboration

It highlights promising efforts around the country that use these approaches. These efforts are not the only ones focusing on education. They are a sample of programs that mirror the issues and goals highlighted in this book. Read on to learn from the experiences, both struggles and successes, of other jurisdictions that are addressing education needs for children in foster care.

DIRECT ADVOCACY

A common question when thinking about education needs of children is "Who is the student's advocate?" For children in foster care, this can be hard to answer. Too often no one is advocating in the school for these children. The following two advocacy programs are working to bring education advocacy to children in foster care. The first grew out of a program that provides representation for children in child abuse and neglect cases. The second is part of the child welfare agency.

The Kathryn A. McDonald Education Advocacy Project (EAP), New York City

In New York City, the Legal Aid Society, Juvenile Rights Division (JRD) represents most children in the child protection system. Based on the pressing needs of these children and through a fellowship from a law firm in 1998, an attorney established a project to provide education advocacy for JRD's child clients. This project has evolved over the past five years and is today known as The Kathryn A. McDonald Education Advocacy Project (EAP).

The EAP is made up of a supervising attorney, a supervising social worker, two paralegals, three attorneys, and a part-time law student. With in-kind support from JRD and funding from outside foundations and individuals, the EAP has tackled three major tasks:

- **Training children's attorneys, agency caseworkers, parents, and foster parents.** The EAP is taking a leading role training on special education needs of children in the child welfare system. Training addresses early intervention and the IDEA Part C process and services for children from birth to age three. It also addresses IDEA Part B advocacy for children from age three through 21.

- **Providing direct educational advocacy for children in the child welfare system.** The EAP receives referrals from many sources, although most come from JRD staff. Efforts are underway to increase referrals from other sources, particularly from agency caseworkers and caregivers. EAP provides direct case advocacy and offers consultation to other child welfare professionals who are tackling education issues. Cases accepted by the EAP are assigned to a paralegal, social worker, or attorney as appropriate. While the EAP's staff is small, efforts are underway to raise funds to hire more staff to serve children in all New York City boroughs.

- **Encouraging collaboration among the many entities affecting a child's education in New York City.** This includes improving communications between the child welfare agency and the Department of Education and the Early Intervention Program, and working with the courts and other legal services and education advocacy providers.

Sidebar 1

Toolkit for Change: A Resource for Education Advocacy Programs

TeamChild, a nonprofit organization in Washington State, with support from Casey Family Programs, created a "Toolkit for Change." This guide provides resources for establishing an education advocacy program in your state. It is based on the successful training and outreach that TeamChild and Casey provided to foster parents, caseworkers, and juvenile courts in Washington. The Toolkit provides:

- templates for training materials;

- brochures;

- comprehensive resource manual for advocates, including user-friendly guidance for advocacy in special education and disciplinary proceedings, and enrollment issues (access the manual online at http://www.teamchild.org/manual.html); and

- instructions on tailoring the material to other states' unique laws and needs, without starting from scratch.

The Toolkit is designed to address a variety of state needs—from initiating trainings for child welfare professionals, to creating direct advocacy programs like those in New York City and Tennessee, described in this chapter.

For more information, e-mail: questions@teamchild.org, or call 206/381-1741.

---

tools. Training by EAP staff is empowering many in the child welfare community to advocate for better education services for youth in care. The community also now knows when to involve the EAP in cases that require their expertise. Expanding the number of trainings has increased the sources of referrals to the program. For example, a recent training for judges and referees in the family court in one of the boroughs resulted in direct referrals from members of the bench there.

- **Highlighting educational services for young children.** Of the cases referred to EAP, 37% are children under age five. The EAP has made training on the developmental issues of young children a major focus of its efforts.

- **Using and recruiting interns and volunteer attorneys from the private bar.** Law students, social work students, and undergraduate interns help alleviate some of the demands on the limited permanent program staff. Volunteer attorneys from the private bar have also been used to assist with the growing cases coming to the attention of the program.

- **EAP staff presence throughout the city increases awareness of legal issues throughout the city's child welfare system.** EAP has staff in three of the five JRD borough offices, with hopes of one day expanding to all five.

Program Contacts

Broward County Interagency Agreement
Andrea Moore
c/o Florida Children First!
6441 East Colonial Drive
Orlando, FL 32807
Phone: 321/206-5760
Fax: 321/206-5765

Debbie Winters
Dependency Court Liaison
Broward County Public Schools
Phone: 754/321-2122
E-mail: debbie.winters@browardschools.com

CA Education Summit and AB 490 Legislation
Miriam Krinsky
Executive Director
Children's Law Center of Los Angeles
(formerly Dependency Court Legal Services, Inc.)
201 Centre Plaza Drive, Suite 10
Monterey Park, CA 91754-2178
323/980-1712
Fax : 323/948-0110
E-mail: krinskym@clcla.org

NYC—The Kathryn A. McDonald Education Advocacy Project
Katherine Locker
The Legal Aid Society
Juvenile Rights Division
199 Water Street, 3rd Floor
New York, New York 10038
Phone: 212/577-3342
E-mail: krlocker@legal-aid.org

Tennessee Education Advocacy
Ann Barker
Assistant General Counsel
Tennessee Department of Children's Services
308 Home Avenue
Maryville, TN 37801
hone: 865/981-5906
E-mail:ann.barker@state.tn.us

Sidebar *2* continued

Cook County Benchmark Hearings
Honorable Patricia Martin Bishop
Child Protection Division
Circuit Court of Cook County
2245 West Ogden Avenue, #8004
Chicago, IL 60612
Phone: 312/433-4756

District of Columbia Benchmark Hearings
The Honorable Juliet McKenna
500 Indiana Ave., N.W.
Washington, DC 20001
Phone: 202/879-0422
E-mail: mckennajj@dcsc.gov

Miami, Florida Young Children Courtroom Interventions
Lynne Katz, Ed.D.
University of Miami, Linda Ray Intervention Center
750 NW 15th Street
Miami, FL 33136
Phone: 305/325-1818
E-mail: lkatz@miami.edu

Challenges

• **Sustaining funding to keep current staff levels, and increasing funding to increase staff** as the numbers of cases brought to the EAP's attention grows.

• **Balancing training goals with direct client advocacy goals.** The amount of training the EAP provides directly affects the number of referrals the project receives. Training and direct advocacy take substantial staff time and resources, and can only increase in relation to staff increases.

Tennessee: Statewide Education Attorneys and Advocates

As a result of a class action lawsuit on behalf of children in the Tennessee foster care system against the state child welfare agency, a consent agreement was reached that addressed educational services for children in care. Under this agreement, the child welfare agency in Tennessee has designated 12 education attorneys and 14 education specialists, one of each assigned to 12 different regions across the state (two regions have two specialists). The education specialists attend individualized education program (IEP) meetings and other school matters when a case manager needs their help and expertise on education issues. The attorneys attend IEP meetings when the school district is represented or the specialist needs legal backup. The specialists and attorneys train caseworkers and other attorneys in the child welfare agency, provide technical assistance to caseworkers when education issues arise, and provide direct advocacy when needed.

- **Early involvement of specialists and/or attorneys has led to quicker and more appropriate services.** Their involvement can raise IDEA issues with the school or court that may prevent a child from coming into custody.
- **Case consultation by attorneys and specialists has increased attention to education issues.** Case managers and other agency staff are excited about having new tools to access educational services for children in their caseload.
- **Educating judges has caused them to ask about education issues when reviewing cases for permanency.** Many judges have begun to recognize the responsibility of the schools to properly discipline or evaluate students before seeking help from the judicial system.
- **Attorneys and specialists have made important regional education contacts.** Part of the role of the education specialists is to meet all the school principals and special education directors within their region. Knowing local players is critical to successful advocacy for children in foster care.

- **Almost all education specialists are former special education teachers,** which uniquely qualifies them to assist with education-related matters.
- **New training requirements.** New caseworkers must receive three hours of education training, and three hours of in-service training each year.

- **Staff turnover.** Despite efforts to provide statewide training, high staff turnover in the child welfare agency makes keeping all current caseworkers trained a challenge.
- **Late referrals.** The specialists and attorneys are at times informed too late of an education need or crisis. Sometimes caseworkers and non-education attorneys fail to spot (in a timely manner) cases that need the expertise of the education staff.

COURTROOM ATTENTION
Benchmark Hearings

Several jurisdictions around the country have implemented benchmark hearings with positive results. These hearings, held in addition to regular reviews and permanency hearings, ensure older youth in foster care are prepared to transition out of foster care. This special hearing helps youth discuss and understand their independence goals. A focus of these hearings is helping youth complete current and plan future educational pursuits.

(1) Cook County, IL

Cook County was the first jurisdiction to start these hearings in the year 2000. The hearings occurred for 14- and 16-year-old children from one residential treatment center with many children in the child welfare system. After success with this limited population, the benchmark hearings were expanded to all children in Cook County, at their 14th and 16th birthdays, and six months before leaving care. These hearings now take up a full five-day–per-week judicial calendar.

Keys to success

- **Special, one-hour hearings.** This scheduling insures adequate time to talk with youth about their options, answer their questions, and address current and future education needs and goals.
- **Active role of caseworker.** Caseworkers notify the youth of hearings, work with them to develop goals, ensure they attend hearings, and invite supportive adults to hearings.
- **Youth prepare information for the hearing.** Youth complete a goal sheet with their caseworkers or other trusted adults. This helps the court find out what education goals the youth has already developed.
- **Youth can invite anyone to the hearing.** This helps identify the adult(s) who will support the youth in the future. This could include a supportive adult with whom the youth connected at school, such as a teacher, counselor, or coach.
- **Involving key agency personnel who are knowledgeable and can make decisions.** For example, a public school liaison attends all benchmark hearings. Cook County already had a public school liaison in the courthouse before the benchmark hearings started.

The liaison now participates in each hearing, provides the child's academic history and relevant information such as attendance and grades, and can be called on to find out additional information for the court. The child welfare agency and the school system share the cost of the liaison, with the court covering some expenses.

- **Binding orders.** Orders from the benchmark hearings are treated as binding agreements, and given the same weight as court orders from other hearings held for the child.

While the benchmark hearings have brought education issues to the forefront of a child's case, this focus should not be limited to these hearings or just one judge.

- **Focus on education can, and should, occur at ALL hearings for a child**. Any judge can use benchmark hearing tools, such as education liaisons and education checklists, any time in a child welfare case. Judges can require that court reports include information about the child's education, and can integrate education issues into their court orders.
- **Judges must understand the education system and what they are requiring caseworkers to do, before they can truly serve clients**. One Cook County judge attended three IEP meetings for a child to ensure the youth's education needs were being served by the school. This kind of effort may not be feasible in all cases due to heavy caseloads and time constraints. However, making such an effort just once may show the school system how serious the court is about addressing education needs, and may improve services for children in care.

(2) Washington, D.C.

Other jurisdictions have recently begun or are considering implementing the Cook County benchmark-hearing model. In Washington, D.C., for example, the benchmark hearing was piloted with one magistrate judge in fall 2003. Unlike Cook County where all youth over 14 are eligible for these hearings, D.C., to stay committed to its one judge/one family model, has made the benchmark hearings only available to youth over age 16 on one judge's calendar. D.C. is planning to evaluate the success of this pilot program, with the possibility of expanding the hearings to other judges' calendars.

Like Cook County, D.C.'s benchmark hearings are recorded. This is important because parents are not entitled to attend hearings in D.C. unless the youth asks them to be present. A transcript can be made available to anyone who requests one, in particular a parent who may not have been invited to the hearing by the child. D.C. also requires the youth's guardian ad litem to submit a report to the court, in addition to the caseworker's report. This report can give the judge greater insight about the youth and makes the benchmark hearings more productive.

Examples of education goals identified for youth in D.C. include: tour or visit college campuses; set a reasonable GPA goal for coming semester; go to school every day; meet with tutor; get involved in extracurricular activities; get a library card; go to a museum; read a book and be prepared to discuss it at the next benchmark hearing.

Challenges

D.C. has faced several challenges while implementing these hearings:

- **Presence of representatives from the school system, child welfare agency, or any other agency** with the knowledge and authority to make decisions about the youth's educational needs and goals. These hearings are a real opportunity to inform children about their future options. Having knowledgeable staff from whatever entity the child may be involved with is critical for the success of these hearings.
- **Time.** Holding individual one-hour hearings for each child, even if part of a large sibling group that traditionally has had one hearing for all children, has created added demands on already packed judicial calendars.

Courtroom Approaches for Young Children: Miami, FL

A Miami judge is bringing research-based early childhood interventions to her community. When families of young children enter the child welfare system, the court orders appropriate assessments and helps them navigate a referral system designed to ensure all young children have a chance to succeed in the future.

The judge's leadership helped establish multidisciplinary collaborative relationships with individuals and community groups who bring child development expertise to the court.[1] This leadership has resulted in:

- Improved assessment tools so the court can have quality evaluations to rely on when making decisions and orders.
- Donations of children's books for court-involved parents to read to their young children.
- Trainings and lecture series for the child welfare community on young children's development and interventions.[2]

The court can now refer children to one of three intervention programs:

- **Mother/infant dyadic therapy:** therapy that treats the mother and infant together, and focuses on their interactions and communications.
- **First juvenile court /Early Head Start program in the country** (which can include the dyadic therapy component).
- **Linda Ray Intervention, University of Miami, program**: works with families with children ages zero to three with prenatal exposure to cocaine.

These interventions are succeeding in several ways:

- **Positive outcomes for young children and families.**
- **Buy-in of legal community.** While some parties, particularly parents' counsel, were hesitant about having their clients consent to these court interventions, the reputation and history of the program's success have swayed many attorneys. These interventions are now believed to be good for all parties in a child welfare case. Testimonials of parents, who have been successfully reunited with their young children, go a long way to endorse the effectiveness of the interventions.

Other courts will hopefully replicate this model in Miami, throughout Florida, and ultimately throughout the country.

LEGISLATION

State legislation can launch statewide improvement by addressing the educational needs of children in foster care. Even when legislative efforts are initially unsuccessful, the attempt at revising state law can bring statewide attention to important issues and lay the groundwork for future amendments.

California AB 490

During the fall 2003 legislative session, the California legislature passed a bill that imposed new duties and rights related to educating children in foster care.[3] This bill sought to build into state law certain provisions from the McKinney-Vento Act, a federal law that addresses the education needs of "homeless children and youth," which may include some children in the child welfare system.[4] While one main objective was to codify into state law the requirement that all children in foster care were entitled to McKinney-Vento type protections, the final bill added more protections and varied from McKinney-Vento in other ways. The bill became effective January 1, 2004.

Highlights of the law

- Allows children in foster care to remain in their school of origin for the remainder of the school year when they are placed outside their home school's boundaries and it is in their best interest to remain in the school of origin.

- Requires the child welfare agency to consider a child's school attendance in foster care placement decisions.
- Designates a foster care education liaison for each local educational agency to oversee placement, transfer, and enrollment issues.
- Allows for immediate enrollment for children in foster care, even before school records, immunizations, or school uniform requirements are satisfied.
- Requires schools to deliver a student's education information and records to a new school placement within two days of receiving a transfer request from the child welfare agency.
- Requires schools to calculate and accept credit for full or partial coursework satisfactorily completed by the student while attending another school.
- Ensures no penalties for absences due to foster care placement changes, court appearances, or related court-ordered activities.[5]

Keys to success

- Involving a supportive state legislator who had political clout and understood the issues.
- Involving key child advocacy groups who could champion the bill. These advocacy groups worked hard to establish universal support from the child welfare community.
- Building consensus outside the child welfare arena. In both child welfare and non-child welfare arenas, consensus-building efforts were critical to address each group's issues with the bill. Substantive changes recommended by outside groups, such as school

systems, were made, as long as they would not compromise the integrity of the bill.

- **Understanding the legislative process, in particular the fiscal impact.** In the eleventh hour, a fiscal analysis from the state's Department of Finance came out that suggested the bill would cost a lot of money. Those working for passage rallied and conducted their own analysis, which showed the fiscal impact of this bill was much smaller than reported by the Department of Finance. (See sidebar #3 for more information about fiscal impact.)

Challenges

- **Transportation funding.** One major issue dropped from the legislation was language requiring the education agency to be solely responsible for funding transportation for children in foster care who remain in their schools of origin. While children under the new law have the right to remain in their home school, the law is silent on which agency will fund the transportation. This issue must be decided on a case-by-case or school-by-school basis. While such a provision would have left less possibility for conflict among the agencies, its inclusion may have caused the bill to fail.
- **Training.** The state department of education has committed to circulating educational materials about the new law to staff. Under the leadership of the Children's Law Center of Los Angeles, several state advocacy groups quickly developed training materials

Fiscal Impact

Fiscal impact is a concern when trying to create new law or policies that will provide more education assistance for children in foster care. Some examples:

California: The fiscal impact attributed to California bill AB 490 almost ruined the chance for passage. The bill's advocates had to create an updated analysis to ensure the bill's survival. The initial fiscal impact attributed to the bill included costs for transportation and other services that were actually required to be paid under other laws, such as Individuals with Disabilities Education Act (IDEA) and the McKinney-Vento Act. The updated analysis pointed out this overstatement and stressed that dollars spent on education for children in foster care could save money for the state in the long run, by ensuring these youth were on the path to future success.

Florida: Broward County, Florida is struggling with a similar issue. The school system has publicly stated a high cost for transporting youth in foster care. This amount is the total cost of transporting each child who is in foster care. The number does not consider that some of these children are entitled to transportation for reasons other than their involvement in foster care, such as eligibility under IDEA, McKinney-Vento, or other state provision. The true cost of providing transportation to keep most children in foster care in their home school is only a portion of the cost stated. However, to obtain an accurate report of the additional expense of transporting youth in foster care who may not otherwise be eligible for transportation requires an in-depth calculation for each child and involves information not typically tracked in school transportation departments.

Getting the numbers right

Despite the difficulties in obtaining accurate information, overstating the cost of services and/or transportation arrangements for children in foster care can damage efforts to help youth in care have better education outcomes. If jurisdictions or states think the cost of assisting this group is overwhelming, well-intentioned school systems may fail to make youth in foster care a priority based on misinformation.

and oversaw training and technical assistance statewide. These groups are also developing training materials for judges, attorneys, caregivers, probation officers, and social workers to ensure the law is applied uniformly and that all parts of the system are aware of the new provisions.

- **Monitoring implementation.** Monitoring how the law's provisions are being implemented will ensure compliance with the law and measure its impact on children in foster care in California. Data to support the benefits of such provisions will assist other states considering similar legislation.

INTERAGENCY COLLABORATION

When child welfare and education agencies work together, they ensure more consistent and targeted services for children in foster care. Meetings, committees, and agreements can create uniform policies within agencies, set procedures for how agencies interact, and designate key staff in each agency to focus on students in foster care.

For a collaboration to succeed, all agencies must agree to commit the time, resources, and staff to tackle key issues. They must identify the issues and decide how to overcome the barriers and make changes. The following two jurisdictions show how child welfare and education agencies can work together to improve education outcomes for children in foster care. The first project has been underway for five years, and shows the benefits of collaborating over time. The second project is just beginning its work and has devised helpful steps for joint planning.

Broward County, FL: Interagency Agreement

In 1998, the School Board of Broward County created a memorandum of understanding on how the county's education and child welfare agencies could improve educational outcomes for children in foster care. While the memorandum of understanding resulted from a threat of a lawsuit on behalf of children in foster care who were not receiving adequate education services, it led to the school and child welfare agency creating the first interagency agreement in 1999.[6] Since that time, dedicated people from the school and child welfare systems have come together at least quarterly to review the agreement and make improvements. A private child welfare provider, ChildNet, has joined the collaboration to manage case services for children in foster care in the county.

Key elements

- **Designated school staff focus on needs of children in foster care.** This includes two liaisons at each school:
  - *A school/child welfare agency liaison,* employed by the school system, serves as the first contact for a child's education information, assists the initial intake and investigation unit of the child welfare agency, and participates in case staffings.
  - *A school/court liaison* attends all shelter hearings; processes special transportation requests; tracks and manages all school-related, court-ordered actions; coordinates activities to help stabilize a student in the educational environment, including notifying the appropriate foster care designee.

In addition, **foster care designees** (usually the guidance counselor) serve as single contact points for that school, assist with registration and transportation, and coordinate activities with other staff, such as special education personnel.

- **Decreasing mobility/increasing stability**. The school system has committed funds for transportation for many of these youth so they can remain in the schools they were attending before being placed in foster care in other neighborhoods.[7] The school has also provided its transportation chart/map to help the child welfare agency predict when transportation will be a challenge and when it can be arranged. In response, the child welfare agency promised to try to keep children near their home school when making placement decisions.

  The agreement also created clear procedures when children in foster care do need to change schools. Several measures also allow the school and agency to subtly communicate about a child's involvement in the child welfare system (e.g., color-coded registration forms and a proposed ChildNet computer system that gives school staff access to a directory of caseworkers with pictures, both designed to eliminate the need to "advertise" the child's involvement in foster care or to wear ID badges when picking up or dropping off child clients).

- **Timely enrollment**. Research in Broward County in January 2003 found many children in foster care were not enrolled timely into school.[8] The participants involved in the interagency agreement made enrollment a priority through a major campaign.[9] As a result, in August 2003, a review on the first day of school revealed that 98% of children in foster care were enrolled, a marked increase from the previous year.

- **Parental decision making (role of parent, foster parent, surrogate parent)**. A tracking system identifies which children in foster care have special education needs. This step has helped ensure surrogate parents are appointed for certain children in foster care with disabilities (chapter 3 provides an in-depth discussion of surrogate parent). Before the agreement, few children in foster care had surrogates appointed, and only a few surrogates were available and trained. With greater attention to identifying children in care with special education needs, efforts are underway to identify which children need surrogates. New avenues for recruiting and training surrogates has led to a pool of almost 50 trained surrogates to serve in this role for almost 200 children.[10]

- **Information sharing**. Confidentiality laws for both agencies create barriers to information sharing.[11] Over the five years of the agreement, information sharing has been achieved within the confines of confidentiality laws. For example, the child welfare agencies provide information to the school system about which children are in foster care, and the school system provides attendance information each week to the child welfare agency to share with caseworkers.

- **Coordinating services**. The agreement has helped link the child welfare agency with IDEA Part C services for children from birth to age three. This has increased screenings, assessments and individualized family service plans (IFSPs) for young children in foster care (chapter 4 details IDEA Part C services). The agreement has also led to coordination of independent living services. For example:

- The school system has identified courses that students in foster care would benefit from, and provided information about them to child welfare agency independent living staff.
- The child welfare and education agencies created a class for youth in care, which is offered outside the traditional school day. It teaches such skills as cooking, sanitation, nutrition, and budgeting. While the child welfare agency and ChildNet provide the funding, the school system recommended a teacher and provided space for the class.
- *Training.* The early years of the agreement focused on training caseworkers and foster care designees. The school and the agencies have developed a procedures manual for caseworkers, and all new workers receive one hour of mandatory preservice training on education needs.[12] Foster care designees attend a yearly training (about 1½ hours), and receive a written guide about their responsibilities.[13] A new e-mail group within the school system allows foster care designees to discuss problems and share ideas. Training has also begun for guardians ad litem and agency attorneys, as well as improved training for the new pool of surrogate parents.

Keys to success

- **Quarterly meetings.** Regular meetings keep the momentum and create an impetus to do more. In addition, subcommittees meet between the quarterly meetings to address specific issues, such as surrogate parents, independent living services, or data collection. Approximately 30 people attend quarterly meetings, with representatives from the school, child welfare agency, and other outside entities.[14] Support from the agency and school leaders and directives to their employees stressing the importance of the meetings, has helped keep meeting attendance strong.

- **Evaluating progress.** Evaluations have helped determine how both agencies are performing under the agreement terms.[15] Recommendations for improvement are incorporated into the terms of the revised agreements. The responses to these recommendations led to the key elements of the agreement, discussed above.

- **Role model for state.** Participants in the Broward County agreement are sharing information about the success of this collaboration with other Florida counties. Legislation[16] passed in the summer of 2004 will bring the successes in Broward County statewide, requiring similar arguments in all counties in Florida.

- **Speaking both languages.** Child welfare and education professionals speak different languages. In Broward County, a strong child advocate with a background in child welfare and education has been involved in this interagency agreement from the start. This advocate has helped bring the agencies together and better understand one another. For example, the term "change in placement" means different things to each agency. Someone who can point out the different interpretations (e.g., a new foster home, a new school place-ment, or some degree of change to a child's education program under IDEA) can alleviate confusion and frustration during the process.

Challenges

- **Improving data accuracy and information exchange.** The child welfare agencies and the school system are working to improve their data systems to enable smooth transfer of information. Before this collaboration, neither entity could determine how many youth in foster care were in the public school system on a given day. That information is now available, although concerns persist about its accuracy.

- **Expanding evaluations to show outcomes for youth.** While evalua-tions have focused attention on issues for the coming year, they have not measured direct outcomes for the children in foster care. A first attempt at learning direct case outcomes resulted in a research brief in 2003, but more data is needed.[17]

- **Institutionalizing reforms.** A method must be created for the reforms to withstand changes in staff and continue over time. Creating these agreements should not depend on one person, office, or entity for survival. Broward is institutionalizing the reforms through the agreement and by creating forms and training materi-als. Because many people are involved in this system, more training and materials are needed.

Los Angeles, CA: County Education Summit

In spring 2003, the Children's Law Center of Los Angeles (CLC) hosted its first "Education Summit" for the Los Angeles, CA area. This summit brought together educators, child welfare experts, advocates, judges, and community leaders to discuss education issues and suggest education reforms for the county's youth in foster care. The summit resulted in general recommendations addressing maintaining school stability for youth in foster care, training and empowering education advocates, and improving coordination of systems. Many specific recommendations were made, such as creating an Education Coordinating Council, a group of key leaders from organizations involved with educating youth in foster care, to coordinate and oversee decisions.[18]

Keys to success

- **Creating a planning committee.** The committee included people from most of the key agencies. This estab-lished buy-in of all entities before the event took place. Two agencies, proba-tion and mental health, were not part of the planning stages, for different reasons, but will be included in the planning of future summits.[19] In the case of mental health, failure to include them in the planning stages resulted in only limited participation by that agency in the summit. As these experi-ences make clear, early involvement in planning helps to establish buy-in and encourages participation.

- **Identifying key topics.** The planning committee identified five key topics[20] before the summit. These were determined after several brainstorming sessions with the committee. Identifying these areas beforehand helped focus the summit on the major issues and avoided wasting time with smaller, irrelevant issues.
- **Involving individuals with decision-making authority.** Involving the presiding judge, the director of the child welfare agency, and top school officials made the summit an event where decisions could be made and agencies and individuals could commit to new approaches and procedures.
- **Addressing issues on many levels.** The summit was not the only activity occurring in the community at the time. New state legislation (see above) and amendments to other administrative policies that would support many of the ideas and changes established at the summit were also underway.
- **Setting realistic goals.** Systemic change is hard. If unreasonable goals are set, all involved become frustrated when change cannot be seen as quickly as hoped. Summit participants tried to be reasonable about the time changes would take, but also pushed to make progress.

Challenges

- **Keeping the information and ideas fresh.** Follow-up summits must provide new information and ideas, and show progress, to continue the momentum from the first summit.
- **Establishing assessment procedures and tools.** Planners need to create a way to measure improvements and determine how well recommendations from the first summit have been implemented.

CONCLUSION

None of these efforts happened overnight. Each developed after a group of committed people decided to make education needs of children in foster care a priority. These approaches may help children in your community or may provide tips and issues to consider when developing a program of your own. All communities need to examine how the education needs of children in foster care are being met, what obstacles exist to receiving a good education, and what approaches should be taken to overcome those barriers. Also critical for all programs are outcome evaluations that show the impact of the innovations on education success for children in foster care.

Endnotes

[1] See Lederman, Cindy S. "Innovations in Assessing and Helping Maltreated Infants and Toddlers in a Florida Court." *Zero to Three* 26(6), June/July 2001, 18.

[2] Ibid., 19.

[3] AB 490 (Information on this new law can be found at http://www.abanet.org/child/rclji/education/ab490.html).

[4] For more information on McKinney-Vento, see chapter 2.

[5] See http://www.abanet.org/child/rclji/education/ab490summary.pdf.

[6] Fla. Stat. Ann. § 39.0016 (2004). A copy of this interagency agreement is available at http://www.abanet.org/child/documents/hb723er.pdf.

7 As of January 2004, the denial rate was less than 5% for special transportation requests. While the school cannot arrange transportation in those small percentage of cases, if other transportation arrangements can be made by the child welfare agency the child could attend the desired school.

8 School Board of Broward County Research Brief, January 2003, found over 12% of children in foster care were not enrolled in school by the 20th day of classes in September 2002. (see http://www.broward. k12.fl.us/research_evaluation/Briefs/brief51-75/ Fostercarebrief67.pdf.) This was three times higher than the rate for the entire student body. After efforts to address this issue, in September 2003, 98% of children in foster care were enrolled by the 20th day, a marked increase from the previous year.

9 The campaign included giving posters and materials to all child welfare service providers, working with caseworkers and supervisors, and providing extra training on strategies to achieve better early enrollment.

10 One such effort involved encouraging members of the Florida bar with experience advocating in the school system to volunteer as surrogates. See Pudlow, Jan. "Lawyers Needed to Serve Children." *Florida Bar News Online*, December 15, 2003. Available at http://www.abanet.org/child/rclji/ education/home.html

11 20 U.S.C. § 1233g; 34 C.F.R. § 99. Family Education Rights Privacy Act (FERPA) dictates the release of educational records.

12 Manual available at http://www.abanet.org/child/rclji/education/ home.html

13 Ibid.

14 School representatives included: court and agency liaisons and a representative foster care designee; representatives from the special education department (including individuals responsible for parent surrogates and Childfind), school social work and psychology department; transportation; adult and community education, information and data system management. Child welfare agency representatives include: state and private agency supervisors for case management divisions; program directors for independent living and placement office; school liaison, and data system personnel. Other representatives come from the guardian ad litem office; legal aid; attorney general's office; private provider agencies (e.g., private shelter facility); and private child advocates.

15 For the most recent evaluation: http://www.broward.k12.fl.us/research_evaluation/ Evaluations/DCFInteragencyEval.pdf.

16 Florida House Bill 279; Senate Bill 1232.

17 Findings included: black students more likely to be placed in foster care; foster care students more likely to be classified as special education eligible for free or reduced lunch, retained within grade at the end of academic year, and begin school year late, less likely to be identified as limited English proficient; and students in foster care received lower standardized test scores than their peers. For complete research brief, see http://www.broward.k12.fl.us/ research_evaluation/Briefs/brief51-75/ Fostercarebrief67.pdf.

18 For detailed recommendations, see http://www.abanet.org/child/rclji/education/ ed_summitrec.pdf

19 Mental health was omitted because of an oversight, and probation was omitted because of the assumption that the summit would only address children in foster care and not children in the delinquency system.

20 The five broad topics were: records access and enrollment issues, academic support and enrichment opportunities, maintaining school stability, literacy, and issues associated with nonpublic schools.

Appendices

Appendix A: General Advocacy Tips and Practitioners' Roles

This summary of practice tips incorporates the advice found throughout this book. When unspecified, the tip applies to ALL advocates. Tips for specific practitioners are found at the end of each section.

☑ Ensure the child is promptly enrolled in an appropriate school setting. (Chapters 1 & 2)

General Tips
- ☐ Advocate for the child to remain in school of origin.
  - ☐ Help identify, with youth's input, placement resources that would keep the child in the same school.
  - ☐ Seek court/agency/school support for placement within the school's jurisdiction.
  - ☐ Help identify transportation options if child is placed outside jurisdiction.
  - ☐ Initiate systemic change to establish right for children in foster care to remain in school of origin (e.g., legislation or interagency agreement).
  - ☐ Use the McKinney-Vento Act, if applicable, by contacting the liaison for your district.
  - ☐ Advocate for immediate enrollment in new school, if placement must change.
  - ☐ Ensure records are transferred and child is enrolled timely at new school.
  - ☐ If child has an IEP, use IDEA procedures to ensure the child's right to a free and appropriate public education (FAPE) is not interrupted (see more on special education below).
  - ☐ Use McKinney-Vento Act, if applicable, by contacting the liaison for your district to establish right to immediate enrollment in a new school.

Specific Roles
- ☐ Judges: Ask at all hearings how a new or change in placement will affect school placement. Consider impact on school placement when determining whether a placement is appropriate.

☑ Access education records and communicate often with the school. (Chapters 1 & 2)

General Tips
- ☐ Determine who the school views as the parent for purposes of consent to release records:
  - ☐ *If the parent*, determine if a parent is maintaining contact with the child's school and/or ensuring the child's education needs are being met; and gain parental consent to access records.

☐ *If the child welfare agency*, obtain education records from agency.

☐ *If the parent is unclear or appropriate party fails to consent*, obtain court order for school to release records.

☐ *If youth is over 18*: Help the youth obtain copies of his education record.

☐ Ensure the child welfare agency includes education records, when available, as part of the case plan.

☐ Ensure records are complete, accurate, and produced timely.

☐ Communicate regularly with school staff who have contact with the child.

Specific Roles

☐ Judges: Order release of education records to appropriate parties. Use your authority to obtain important information about a child promptly. Use your court education liaison, if one exists, to obtain information about a child.

☐ Caseworkers: Share available education records with foster care providers as required under federal law.

☐ Parent attorneys: Advocate for parent clients to retain the right to access records and communicate with the school until parental rights are terminated or another court order or state law restricts your right to do so.

☑ Ensure child receives quality education services and programs. (Chapters 1 & 2)

General Tips

☐ Know what services are available in the school and make efforts to get and keep these services in place for the child. Make sure the child welfare system provides other needed education services.

☐ Know what the No Child Left Behind Act requires. Know how your state defines "annual yearly progress" or "persistently dangerous."

☐ Find out which schools in your jurisdiction have been identified as "in need of improvement" and advocate for transfers (if two consecutive years) and/or supplemental services (if three consecutive years) for the child's specific circumstance.

☐ Find out which schools in your jurisdiction have been identified as "persistently dangerous" and advocate for transfers for the child's specific circumstance.

Specific Roles

☐ Child welfare agencies: Focus on what programs the schools lack, and find or establish new programs in the community or in your agency to fill gaps.

☐ Judges: Order the child welfare agency to provide specific services for the child (e.g., tutoring or mentoring) if they are warranted in the child welfare case. Order advocates to pursue services and/or transfers through the school system.

☑ **Obtain special education services for appropriate children.**
   (Chapters 1, 2, & 3)

General Tips
- ☐ Identify children in foster care with disabilities, both diagnosed and undiagnosed.
- ☐ Understand the benefits afforded under IDEA and pursue advocacy within the school system.
- ☐ Make written referrals to begin the special education identification process for appropriate children.
- ☐ Advocate for quality evaluations to be conducted when assessment information is not already available.
- ☐ Determine who is the education decision maker for the child.
- ☐ Determine if a surrogate parent is needed, and if so ensure an appropriate individual is appointed. Encourage individuals involved with the child to be appointed as surrogate.
- ☐ Get involved in the school system's IEP process to ensure a child in foster care is identified accurately, receives appropriate services, and is placed in appropriate, not overly restrictive, education settings.
- ☐ Ensure transition services under IDEA (starting at age 14) are being coordinated with youth's transition services through the child welfare system.
- ☐ File formal written complaints with the state department of education, if appropriate.
- ☐ Seek outside support of education experts and/or attorneys for assistance with mediation and due process.

Specific Roles
- ☐ Caseworkers and child advocates/attorneys: Talk with the child, in a developmentally appropriate manner, to discuss the child's feelings about the disability and possible special education services.
- ☐ Attorneys for all parties: Ask judges to order assessments, which will be used to speed the school identification process and clarify education decision-making authority. Supply the school with assessment documentation.
- ☐ Caseworkers: Supply the school with documentation, such as confirmation of physical and mental health diagnosis.
- ☐ Judges: Help determine who has education decision-making authority so the issue will not delay school services.
- ☐ Child welfare agencies: Recruit and train foster parents and others (but not child welfare agency employees) to be the education decision maker. This ensures that knowledgeable people are making education decisions.

☑ **Obtain Section 504 services for appropriate children with disabilities. (Chapters 2 & 3)**

General Tips
☐ Determine how your jurisdiction decides decision-making authority under Section 504 when a child is in foster care.
☐ Understand and advocate for services and protections under Section 504 for children with disabilities.
☐ Remember to consider Section 504 eligibility for children with disabilities found ineligible for IDEA services and protections.

☑ **Ensure discipline measures are appropriate. (Chapters 1, 2, & 5)**

General Tips
☐ Before discipline occurs, request a school meeting to discuss interventions that will help the child's behavior improve. Work with other child welfare system advocates to explore techniques the school can use to interact with the child, such as positive reinforcement and behavior modification models.
☐ Consider how the child feels about sharing details of foster care involvement with the school. Would sharing the private information about the child cause unfair treatment?
☐ Ensure child's involvement in foster care is considered when appropriate. Does the school disciplinarian understand the child's situation and how child welfare involvement may have contributed to misbehavior or misconduct?
☐ Know your state laws and school district discipline policies. Keep a copy of the policies for each child's school district.
☐ If discipline is necessary, suggest alternatives that will not interfere with the child's educational progress (e.g., afterschool volunteer work, weekend community projects).
☐ If the school district has a zero-tolerance policy, examine the policy to determine if the school has discretion to follow through with a sanction. If there is discretion, argue the facts of the case and present the child's circumstances at the disciplinary hearing.
☐ Prepare for disciplinary hearings by obtaining supporting documentation from others involved in the child's life that may be persuasive to the hearing officer (e.g., coach, teacher, therapist, caseworker, foster parent).
☐ Ensure the child understands the disciplinary process and understands what rules he or she is accused of violating (e.g., Did the child recently transfer to this school, and does the discipline policy differ from the last school? Was the student ever provided a copy of the new disciplinary code?).
☐ Pursue appeals when warranted. While there are limited appeal avenues for suspensions under 10 days, appeals are usually options to challenge long-term suspensions and expulsions.
☐ If the child was also arrested for the act that led to the suspension, be aware of the interplay between the suspension hearing process and the court process. Coordinate activities with the child's attorney in the delinquency or criminal matter.

☑ **Ensure discipline measures for children with disabilities are appropriate. (Chapters 1, 2, & 5)**

General Tips

☐ Advocate for and review Functional Behavior Assessments (FBAs) and Behavioral Intervention Plans (BIPs) when appropriate, and determine if they are addressing specific behavioral issues. Advocate for the creation of a BIP before a discipline problem develops.

☐ Ensure a child in special education is not suspended more than 10 days (including cumulative, if pattern of removal) without the school holding a manifestation meeting. If the school does not schedule this required manifestation meeting on its own, request the meeting in writing.

☐ Ensure the parent, person acting as the parent, or the surrogate parent has notice of the meeting and attends.

☐ Ensure the manifestation meeting addresses: Was there an appropriate IEP? Was it being implemented? Was there a nexus between the behavior and the disability?

☐ Request a manifestation hearing for a child who lacks an IEP if you think the school knew, or should have known the child had a disability that was having an educational impact.

☐ If the child is placed in an interim alternative education setting (IAES), ensure the child's IEP is still being implemented.

☐ Ensure a child with an IEP who is suspended or expelled (e.g., no nexus between behavior and disability) still receives a free appropriate public education.

☐ Ensure that a disabled child in foster care who violates the disciplinary code, but has not yet been found IDEA eligible, does not receive unnecessary and/or inappropriate punishments.

☐ Check that delinquency petitions are not being adjudicated for issues that should be addressed in a school setting and through appropriate school programming.

☐ Ensure the school has provided special education and disciplinary records with reports to law enforcement about a child with special education needs.

Specific Roles

☐ Attorneys and caseworkers: Attend and advocate for the child at manifestation hearings and other meetings and hearings related to discipline. Even though you are not the legal decision maker, you can provide information to the team that may affect the ultimate team decision.

☐ Parent or surrogate: If you disagree with the team decision following a manifestation hearing, or with decisions about placing a child in an IAES, you can appeal through an expedited due process hearing.

☑ **Keep older youth in school. (Chapters 1 & 2).**

General Tips

☐ Encourage youth to complete high school.

☐ Know the laws in your state regarding the age children are required to be in school and the age children have the right to be in school.

☐ Know how Chafee funds can be used in your state. Advocate using these funds to help older youth in your community complete high school and pursue further education. Encourage developers of your state Chafee plan to creatively use funds to support education goals for youth.

☐ Discuss further education options with youth and help youth identify further education plans. Seek court or parent reinforcement of need for future planning, if appropriate. Never assume someone else has had the conversation.

☐ Encourage youth interested in higher education to take college entrance exams. Ensure they have transportation to these exams and advocate for financial assistance for exams and preparatory classes.

☐ Educate youth, and other child welfare professionals, on availability of grants, scholarships, and tuition waiver programs, including the availability of education and training vouchers.

☐ Request vocational assessments and transition planning from the child welfare agency for all youth. Ensure the IEP teams develops vocational assessments and transition plans for teens in special education.

☐ Inform youth of their additional education rights upon turning 18 years old.

☑ **Ensure young children are enrolled in appropriate education programs. (Chapters 1, 2, & 4)**

General Tips

☐ Learn about the care and education programs in your community and advocate for programs that will meet the needs of each young child. Push for early identification, thorough assessments, and appropriate services and program placements.

☐ Make sure the young child has a "medical home"; that the child is seen regularly by a treating physician who knows her medical history and ensures she receives evaluations, treatment, and follow-up. Make sure parents are informed of medical information, diagnosis, and treatment and consulted about the child's medical history.

☐ Learn about child development to improve your understanding of healthy development and ability to spot problems.

☐ Ensure a young child in foster care is enrolled by his primary doctor in an EPSDT program. Seek court orders to enforce a child's right to EPSDT services. Be sure that all facets of EPSDT are being provided—screening, diagnosis, and treatment.

☐ Advocate for enrollment in Head Start or Early Head Start for an eligible child. Determine if foster care involvement allows for special eligibility status.

127

- [ ] Determine if young children in foster care are eligible for infant and toddler services under IDEA Part C. If so, initiate referrals with the school system or other Part C entity to obtain these services.
  - [ ] Determine who is the education decision maker, be it the parent or other individual. If a surrogate parent is needed, ensure that an appropriate and knowledgeable individual is appointed.
  - [ ] Know how your state defines developmental delay and whether your state includes the "at risk" of developmental delay category for eligibility under Part C.
  - [ ] Attend meetings that address eligibility under Part C and development of IFSPs, and continue to monitor implementation.
  - [ ] Ensure smooth transitions from Part C to preschool services by age three.
- [ ] For children over three who have not been receiving Part C services, begin the referral and evaluation process under Part B.
  - [ ] Determine if the child's school system permits developmental delay as a category of disabilities under Part B for children over three.
  - [ ] Help draft the child's IEP (or IFSP if applicable) and ensure appropriate services and placement are identified.
  - [ ] Continue to monitor service delivery during these young, critical years, and ensure appropriateness of programs and services.

Specific Roles

- [ ] Judges: Ask about relevant information related to healthy development for young children at all hearings (e.g., whether developmental and mental health screenings have been completed and whether enrollments in early childhood programs have been arranged). Order parties to make Part C referrals for all children birth to age three who may require services.
- [ ] Caseworkers: Establish procedures to make Part C referrals for children from birth to age three with substantiated abuse and neglect administrative findings.

Additional Reading:

Yu, Elisabeth, Pamela Day & Millicent Williams. *Improving Educational Outcomes for Youth in Care: Symposium Summary Report.* Washington, D.C.: Child Welfare League of America, 2002.

Christian, Steve. "Educating Children in Foster Care." Children's *Policy Initiative,* December 2003.

Casey Family Programs. *A Road Map for Learning: Improving Educational Outcomes in Foster Care.* Seattle, WA: Casey Family Programs, 2004.

Green, Sarah & Laurie E. Powers. *Are We Ignoring Foster Youth With Disabilities?* Portland, OR: Fostering Futures Project, Spring 2003.

McMillen, Curtis, et al. « Educational Experience and Aspirations of Older Youth in Foster Care." *Child Welfare* 82, July/August 2003, 475 – 495.

Burrell, Sue. *Getting Out of the "Red Zone": Youth From the Juvenile Justice and Child Welfare System Speak Out About the Obstacles to Completing Their Education, and What Could Help.* San Francisco, CA: Youth Law Center, April 2003.

Litchfield, Melissa, et al. "Improving Educational Outcomes for Youth in Foster Care: Perspectives From Judges and Program Specialists." *Technical Assistance Bulletin* 6, June 2002.

Make a Difference in a Child's Life: A Manual for Helping Children and Youth Get What They Need in School. Seattle, WA: TeamChild & Casey Family Programs, December 2001.

Toolkit for Change: A Guide to Starting an Educational Advocacy Project in Your State. Seattle, WA: TeamChild & Casey Family Programs, 2002.

Seyfried, et al. "Assessing the Educational Outcomes of Children in Long-Term Foster Care: First Findings." *School Social Work Journal* 24, Winter 2000, 68–88.

Appendix C: IDEA Regulations

Excerpts from federal education laws and regulations have been compiled as an external, internet resource to accompany this book. Readers who are interested in reviewing the full text of federal laws and regulations referred to in this book are encouraged to locate this resource at http://www.abanet.org/child/rclji/education/.

Excerpts from the following are included:
- Individuals with Disabilities Education Act (law and regulations)
- Section 504 of the Rehabilitiation Act (law and regulations)
- Family Education Rights and Privacy Act (law and regulations)
- McKinney-Vento Act (law)
- No Child Left Behind Act (law)

Ronald S. Palomares, PhD, American Psychological Association

What is a psychological test?

It is a measurement device or technique used to understand and predict behavior. It is often used to help understand how likely someone will behave in a certain manner. Typical administration methods are:

- **Individual test**—a test given to one person at a time.
- **Group test**—a test given to more than one person at a time.

What are the various types of psychological tests?

- **Ability test**—These contain items that can be scored in terms of speed (how fast do you finish it), accuracy (how many do you get done correctly), or both (how fast and correct). An example of the latter combined is a typing test, where both speed and accuracy is most important.
- **Achievement test**—These tests measure previous learning. For example, a history test where one is asked to respond with names and dates of historical events.
- **Aptitude test**—These tests measure the potential for learning or acquiring a specific skill. For example, a test that measures one's desire to become a writer by evaluating understanding and thoughts about the writing profession to see if they coincide with successful writers.
- **Intelligence test**—These tests measure a person's general potential to think abstractly and to solve problems, especially by adapting to changing circumstances.

- **Personality test**—These tests measure typical behavior (e.g., traits, temperaments, and dispositions) of a person. They focus on identifying an individual's tendency to show a particular behavior or response to various situations. Two subtypes of personality tests are:
  - *Structured Personality Test*—A personality test designed in an objective manner, usually comprised of true/false responses, and has expected types of responses.
  - *Projective Personality Test*—A personality test that usually has some type of stimulus (for example an inkblot) and the expected responses are ambiguous.
- **Standardized Interview**—This is an interview conducted under well-defined conditions. Usually involves asking specific questions in a defined order.

What is an assessment?

Assessments are used to evaluate an individual's current and future functioning using a variety of tests.

What are the various types of assessments?

- **Behavioral Assessment**—focuses on the behaviors, thoughts (cognitions) or physiological responses that define the disordered condition.
- **Diagnostic Assessment**—a detailed evaluation of an individual's strengths and weaknesses in a variety of areas.

131

- **Psychological Assessment**—behaviors are measured against a normal standard and classified into categories, underlying causes of behaviors are determined based on the results from several different tests.
- **Progress Evaluation Assessment**—charts day-to-day or week-to-week progress of the individual in a particular area.
- **Screening Assessment**—a relatively brief examination to identify if the individual is eligible for a certain program or has a disorder that requires further evaluation.

What tests are typically used to assess special education handicapping conditions?

Most psychological assessments will include the following:
- Student interview
- Teacher interview
- Parent/guardian interview (in person or by telephone)
- Classroom observation
- Record review (school, medical, and other relevant records made available to the psychologist)

In addition to the standard measures listed above, the following handicapping conditions and tests may be included as part of the psychological assessment:
- Severe Learning Disabilities (LD)
  - Achievement
  - Cognitive/Intelligence (IQ)
- Severe Emotional Disturbance (SED)
  - Achievement
  - Cognitive/Intelligence (IQ)
  - Behavior
  - Personality

- Mental Retardation (MR)
  - Cognitive/Intelligence (IQ)
  - Adaptive Abilities
- Other Health Impaired (OHI)—specific to suspected Attention-Deficit Hyperactivity Disorder (ADHD)
  - Achievement
  - Cognitive/Intelligence (IQ)
  - Behavior

(NOTE: A psychological evaluation is highly specific for each student, based on their individual needs and the reason they were referred for the evaluation. The decisions made in the selection of assessment instruments used are based upon these factors. The above list is an example of tests that may be used in the various situations.)

Test Review Resource

The **Buros Institute of Mental Measurements** (http://www.unl.edu/buros/) has a history of reviewing commercially available psychological, educational, and similar types of tests since 1938. The Institute publishes the Mental Measurement Yearbook and Tests in Print series, which contains critical reviews of a test by two or more respected researchers. Each review includes general information about the test (including publisher, who can administer the test, technical properties) and information about the test's shortcomings and strengths. Some information is technical, yet each review presents a critical analysis of the test that many lay individuals will find useful.

(NOTE: Test reviews can be found in one of the two Institute-published books, available at most higher education libraries. In addition, reviews can be purchased individually through the Institute's website.)

Test Publishing Companies

The following companies develop and publish assessment instruments that measure many aspects of human behavior, attitudes, and personality, as well as related resources (e.g., books, software, etc.). Each company has an expanded description of the tests they sell, including uses and who can administer them.

American Guidance Service (AGS), Circle Pines, Minnesota
http://www.agsnet.com/
Web resource entitled: Glossary of Common Test Terms
http://www.agsnet.com/glos/

Psychological Corporation (PsychCorp), San Antonio, Texas
http://www.psychcorp.com
Home page focuses on psychological assessment tools:
http://marketplace.psychcorp.com/
PsychCorp.com/Cultures/en-US/
Psych+Community/

Riverside Publishing; Itasca, Illinois
http://www.riverpub.com/
Web resource entitled: Glossary of Testing, Measurement and Statistical Terms:
http://www.riverpub.com/scoring/
glossary/default.jsp

Western Psychological Services (WPS), Los Angeles, California
http://www.wpspublish.com

Additional Resources
American Psychological Association
http://www.apa.org/science/testing.html
This link provides information related to frequently asked questions about testing, as well as resources related to standards for educational and psychological testing.

ETS Test Collection
http://www.ets.org/testcoll/index.html
This collection of over 20,000 tests provides minimal information on each test, but does provide test author and publisher names and, in some instances, an abstract briefly describing the test.

Professors Dumont/Willis
http://alpha.fdu.edu/psychology/
Psychology professors at Fairleigh Dickinson University have put together a resource page with links to numerous reviews and information about psychological tests and assessment. (The above link is to their Test Reviews and Comments page.)

Commonly Used Tests and Assessment Batteries
Note: Test publishers appear at the end of each test description. Refer to "Test Publishing Companies" for further information.

Achievement Test examples:
Kaufman Test of Educational Achievement, 2d Edition (K-TEA II)
An achievement test for individuals between the ages of $4\frac{1}{2}$ and 90 that assesses skills in reading, math, written language, and oral language. (AGS)

Peabody Individual Achievement Test-Revised/Normative Update (PIAT-R/NU)

An achievement test for children between age five and 23, assessing six content areas: general knowledge, reading recognition, reading comprehension, mathematics, spelling, and written expression. (AGS)

Wechsler Individual Achievement Test, 2d Edition (WIAT-II)

Assesses the achievement of students age four to 85. It measures a student's achievement across an extensive range of academic areas. (PsychCorp)

Wide Range Achievement Test, 3d Edition (WRAT-3)

Measures reading, spelling, and arithmetic skills in individuals between age five and 75. (WideRange.com)

Woodcock-Johnson III Tests of Achievement (WJ III)

The Standard Battery of the WJ-III Achievement has 12 subtests that provide a broad set of academic achievement scores for individuals between age two and 90. An additional 10 tests (Extended Battery) provides in-depth diagnostic information on a wider range of academic strengths and weaknesses. (Riverside)

Behavior Assessment—Behavior Rating Scales examples:
Attention Deficit Disorders Evaluation Scale (ADDES)

This school version of the scale, used with children ages four to 20, was designed to provide a measure of Attention Deficit Disorders: inattention, impulsivity and hyperactivity. (Hawthorne)

Behavior Assessment System for Children (BASC)

The BASC is a multimethod and multi-dimensional approach to evaluating the behavior and self perceptions of children age four to 18. The system includes a self-report scale (completed by the student), a rating scale for parents and a rating scale for teachers. It measures numerous aspects of behavior and personality. (AGS)

Child Behavior Checklist (CBCL) and Teacher Rating Form (TRF)

The CBCL and TRF are checklists and questionnaires for children age two to 18. It is completed by the student's parent or teacher regarding behaviors exhibited by the child. (Achenbach)

Conners' Rating Scales—Revised

Brief questionnaires completed by parents and teachers, focusing on attention, impulsivity, and social problems associated with ADHD and intended for ages three to 17. (Multi-Health Systems—mhs.com)

Vineland Adaptive Behavior Scales (VABS)

VABS—Classroom Edition—questionnaire completed by teachers VABS—Survey and Expanded Interview Forms—questionnaire completed by an evaluator working with a parent or other caretaker. Both pieces focus on evaluating an individual across the domains of communication, daily living skills, and socialization and, for younger students, motor skills. (AGS)

Intelligence Test examples:
Test of Nonverbal Intelligence, 3d Edition (TONI-3)
Designed to be a language-free measure of intellectual ability for individuals age six to 90. (AGS)

Stanford-Binet Intelligence Scales, 5th Edition (SB 5)
Assesses intelligence and cognitive abilities of individuals between age two and 90. (Riverside)

Wechsler Intelligence Scale for Children, 4th Edition (WISC-IV)
Measures intellectual abilities of children between age six and 17. (PsychCorp)

Wechsler Adult Intelligence Scale, 3d Edition (WAIS-III)
Measure intellectual abilities of adolescents and adults age 16 through 89. (PsychCorp)

Woodcock Johnson III Tests of Cognitive Abilities (WJ-III)
Assesses general intellectual abilities of individuals age two to 90. (Riverside)

Memory and Visual Motor Skills examples:
Bender Visual Motor Gestalt Test, 2d Edition (Bender)
The Bender is often the first test used in an extended psychological assessment because it is a nonthreatening warm-up that also assesses visual-motor development (eye-hand coordination) and can screen for neuropsychological impairments. (Riverside)

Test of Memory and Learning (TOMAL)
Evaluates general and specific memory functions, including verbal and nonverbal memory, as well as delayed recall, of children and adolescents between age five and 20. (AGS)

Children's Memory Scale (CMS)
Evaluates memory functions focused around memory, learning and attention in children and adolescents between age five and 16. (PsychCorp)

Wechsler Memory Scales, 3d Edition (WMS-III)
The WMS-III is for adolescents and adults (ages 16-89 years) and used to evaluate general memory, and a variety of memory functions including visual memory, auditory memory, and working memory. (PsychCorp)

Personality Tests—Projective examples
Storytelling tests:
- Children's Apperception Test and the Thematic Apperception Test
  The student is shown a set of pictures and asked to create a story based on the pictures.

Drawing tests:

- Draw-A-Person

  The student draws a picture of a person and is asked a series of questions about it.

- House-Tree-Person

  Similar to the Draw-A-Person, the student is asked to draw a picture of a house, a picture of a tree, and one of a person. The student is then asked questions about the drawings.

- Kinetic Family Drawing

  The student draws a picture of a family and is asked a series of questions about it.

Other example of projective test:

- Incomplete Sentence Blank

  The student is asked to complete a series of incomplete sentences, such as "I like ____."

Personality Tests—Structured examples

- Millon Adolescent Personality Inventory (MAPI)

  A self-report test comprised of 150 true/false items used to assess personality characteristics of adolescents between age 13 and 18. (Pearson Assessments—pearsonassessments.com)

- Personality Inventory for Children, 2d Edition (Pic-2)

  Gathers information from the parent about the student's personality and adjustment. The PIC-2 is comprised of 275 true/false items and is used for children and adolescents between the five and 19. (WPS)

136

About the Author

Kathleen McNaught, J.D., is an Assistant Director of the National Child Welfare Resource Center on Legal and Judicial Issues, part of the American Bar Association Center on Children and the Law. Ms. McNaught brings both the child and parent representation perspectives to this Resource Center through seven years of practicing law in Maryland. In her current position she has provided training and technical assistance on the Adoption and Safe Families Act and the Children and Family Services Review process. Ms. McNaught also provides training and technical assistance around the country on the education needs of children in foster care. Before joining the ABA, she was a staff attorney for three years for Maryland's Legal Aid Bureau in its child advocacy unit, and an attorney in private practice for four years, representing parents and children in child welfare cases, as well as in education, delinquency and custody matters. She received her J.D. from The American University, Washington College of Law in 1994, and her B.A. from Franklin and Marshall College in 1991.

INDEX

Section 504 of the
Rehabilitation Act
(Section 504): 11, 17, 18,
24, 25, 26, 38, 96, 97, 99,
125, 130
service coordinator: x, 71,
73, 74
short-term suspensions: 25,
90, 95, 97
signing the IEP: 60
special education: vii, viii, ix,
xi, 8, 9, 11, 13, 14, 17, 23,
24, 31, 32, 35, 36, 37, 38,
39, 40, 41, 42, 43, 44, 45,
46, 47, 48, 49, 50, 51, 53,
54, 55, 56, 57, 58, 59, 61,
62, 63, 73, 75, 76, 79, 83,
92, 93, 96, 97, 98, 100,
101, 104, 105, 108, 115,
119, 122, 124, 126, 127,
132
special education services:
vii, 11, 17, 24, 32, 35, 36,
37, 39, 43, 45, 50, 58, 61,
62, 63, 75, 79, 83, 92, 93,
96, 97, 98, 124

standards of representation: 8
statement of transition
services: xi, 58, 59
stigma: 90
supplementary aids and
services: ix, x, 58
surrogate parent: xi, 5, 24,
30, 42, 43, 44, 53, 56, 57,
64, 70, 75, 76, 78, 80, 81,
99, 115, 124, 126, 128
suspension: xi, 8, 25, 26, 27,
89, 90, 91, 92, 95, 96, 97,
98, 99, 101, 125

T

tape recording: 60
timely enrollment: 115
transfer of rights at 18: 31
transistion service: x, xi, 23,
48, 57, 58, 68, 69, 124
transition plan: xi, 49, 57,
59, 79, 127
transportation: ix, xi, 27, 28,
30, 62, 67, 74, 112, 113,
114, 115, 119, 122, 127
tuition waivers: 30, 31

W

well-being: 2, 3, 14, 18
wrong disability: 61

Y

young children: vii, 6, 7, 14,
15, 19, 28, 29, 30, 31, 55,
65, 66, 67, 68, 69, 70, 71,
73, 74, 75, 77, 78, 79, 81,
82, 83, 84, 85, 87, 105,
107, 110, 111, 115, 127,
128

Z

zero tolerance: 17, 25, 32, 93,
95, 101